SECURED TRANSACTIONS

by
Steven Emanuel
Harvard Law School, J.D. 1976

emanuel law outlines

Secured Transactions, Fourth Edition, Copyright © 1988 by Steven L. Emanuel
Emanuel Law Outlines, Inc. • 1865 Palmer Avenue • Larchmont, NY 10538

Abbreviations Used in Text

C&K—Countryman and Kaufman, *Commercial Law, Cases and Materials* (Little, Brown, 1971)

Coogan—Coogan, Hogan & Vagts, *Bender's Uniform Commercial Code Service—Secured Transactions* (Matthew Bender, 1980)

F&H—Farnsworth and Honnold, *Commercial Law, Cases and Materials* (Foundation Press, 4th Ed., 1985)

Gilmore—Grant Gilmore, *Security Interest in Personal Property* (Little, Brown, 2 Vols., 1965)

Henson—Ray Henson, *Secured Transactions* (West Hornbook Series, 2nd Ed., 1979)

Nutshell—David Epstein, *Debtor and Creditor Relations in a Nutshell* (West Nutshell Series, 1973)

SS&W—Speidel, Summers & White, *Commercial Law* (West Publ., 4th Ed., 1987)

W&S—White and Summers, *Uniform Commercial Code Handbook* (West Publ., 2nd Ed., 1980)

TABLE OF CONTENTS

SCOPE AND PURPOSE OF ARTICLE 9

FORMAL REQUISITES OF A SECURITY INTEREST

PERFECTION

PERFECTION IN MULTI-STATE TRANSACTIONS

PRIORITIES

DEFAULT

SCOPE AND PURPOSE OF ARTICLE 9

I. NATURE OF SECURITY INTERESTS

A. Plight of unsecured creditors: Suppose Borrower wants a loan from Lender. Lender might make an *unsecured* loan, that is, a loan on default of which Lender would not have the right to foreclose against specific property of Borrower. The only way Lender could get his money back if Borrower did not voluntarily pay would be to sue Borrower, get a money judgment against him, and then have the sheriff levy against Borrower's assets. But this might take a long time, and would involve legal fees. Furthermore, if Borrower went bankrupt, Lender would be no better off than any other unsecured creditor, and would have to share *pro rata* with these other unsecured creditors.

   1. Rights of secured creditor: If, however, Lender had made a *secured* loan to Borrower, he would be better off when Borrower defaulted. In making a secured loan, Borrower would sign a *security agreement* stating that on default, Lender would be entitled to take possession of specified *collateral* owned by Borrower. Lender would then simply have to take the collateral, and then sell it, rather than having to sue Borrower for a personal judgment.

      a. Bankruptcy: Moreover, if Lender has a secured loan, he will be much better off in the event of Borrower's bankruptcy. Lender will not have to share *pro rata* with all the other unsecured creditors; instead, he will be able to take possession of the collateral just as if there had been no bankruptcy. His chances of receiving payment of a sizeable portion of his debt are thus much greater than if he were an unsecured creditor.

B. Article 9's scope: Security interests in *personal property* (i.e., non-real estate) are governed by Article 9 of the Uniform Commercial Code. That Article sets forth not only the procedure for creating and administering security interests, but also sets forth the rights of holders of security interests as against unsecured creditors, except where the Federal Bankruptcy Act preempts the field.

II. SCOPE OF ARTICLE 9 GENERALLY

A. Pre-UCC law: Under pre-UCC law, a great variety of devices existed for assuring the repayment of debt. Each of these devices (pledge, chattel mortgage, trust receipt, conditional sale, etc.) had its own rules with respect to the secured party's (that is, the secured lender's) rights against the debtor and against third parties, with respect to the debtor's rights against third parties, and with respect to requirements for giving *public notice* of security interests. Major differences existed not only among the various methods, but among the various states with respect to a given method. Many of these differences no longer served a useful function by the time the UCC was proposed.

B. UCC supersedes previous legislation: The UCC, which has become the law of 49 states since it was first enacted by Pennsylvania in 1953, supersedes all legislation dealing with the various individual security devices. Although the devices themselves are still allowable, the general rules of Article 9 apply to them, and for all practical purposes, there is only one device, a "*security interest*", under Article 9.

   1. Distinctions within Article 9: However, Article 9 does make certain distinctions among various security interests, depending on the nature of the collateral, the kind of loan made or credit given, the business of the debtor, etc. For example, the "public notice" requirements in a case where the lender takes possession of the collateral are different from the requirements where the debtor continues in possession of the collateral. Thus although there is only one "security interest", some of the pre-UCC distinctions survive. (See Comment to §9-101. See also W&S, 756).

C. 1972 Amendments to Article 9: The UCC was not truly "uniform" by the time it was enacted by the various states — for instance, by 1966 47 of the 54 sections of Article 9 had been altered by at least one state. To regain some of the lost uniformity of Article 9, and to remedy some of the practical defects of the Article, a series of amendments was proposed in 1971 by an official Article 9 Review Committee.

   1. New official 1972 text: The Review Committee's amendments were incorporated in 1972 into a *new official text* of Article 9. As of 1988, all but five states (Alaska, Louisiana, Missouri, South Carolina and Vermont) had adopted the 1972 version. The others have kept the original version (except Louisiana, which has not enacted Article 9 at all).

   2. Our focus: *All references, unless otherwise indicated, are to the 1972 Code.* Where there are important differences between the 1972 version and the 1962 version, the 1962 version is cited as "1962 Code §9-__".

D. General application of Article 9: Article 9 applies to "any transaction (regardless of its form) which is intended to create a security interest in personal property or fixtures including goods, documents, instruments, general intangibles, chattel paper or accounts." §9-102(1)(a).

   1. Applicable to certain sales: Article 9 governs not only security interests, but also certain *sales*, namely, sales of *accounts* and *chattel paper*. The meaning of each of these categories, and the reason for including sales of these items within the scope of Article

9, will be discussed *infra*, pp. 47 and 50. See §9-102(1)(b).

2. **Consensual security interests:** Article 9 applies only to ***consensual*** security interests in personal property and fixtures. Consensual security interests are those negotiated and expressly agreed to by the parties, as distinguished from ***statutory*** security interests.

   a. **Statutory liens excluded:** Statutory security interests (often called ***statutory liens***) are granted by various state laws to certain classes of persons (garagemen, hotel keepers, repairmen, etc.) — these statutory liens, which come into force ***whether the parties agree to them or not*** — are expressly excluded from the scope of Article 9 by §9-102(2). (The only time Article 9 applies at all to statutory liens is for the purpose of calculating certain priorities under §9-310.)

3. **Common law liens excluded:** Common law liens, like statutory liens, are not within the scope of Article 9 security interests. See §9-104(c) — "a lien given by statute or other rule of law for services or materials . . . " is excluded; the term "other rule of law" presumably applies to common law, although the text of the Code does not so state. See Comment 3, §9-104.

4. **Other excluded transactions:** Since the overall purpose of Article 9 was to cover all security interests and certain sales, the Draftsmen felt it necessary to then specifically exclude certain transactions that have nothing to do with commercial financing. Thus §9-104 excludes from the scope of Article 9 the following, among other items:

   a. a ***landlord's*** lien (§9-104(b))

   b. a ***statutory*** lien for services or materials (see *supra*; §9-104(c))

   c. a sale of accounts or chattel paper as part of a ***sale of the business out of which they arose*** (§9-104(f))

   d. an assignment of accounts or chattel paper which is for the purpose of ***collection*** only (*Id.*)

   e. the transfer of a right to payment under a contract to an ***assignee*** who is also to ***perform*** under the contract (*Id.*)

   f. the transfer of a single account to an assignee in whole or part satisfaction of prior debt

   g. the transfer of certain interests under an ***insurance policy*** (§9-104(g))

   h. any interest in or lien on ***real estate***, including a ***lease*** of or rents for real estate. (§9-104(j)) (An exception is the provision in §9-313 for fixtures, which have some of the qualities of personal property and some of the characteristics of real estate. See *infra*, p. 117.)

  i. the transfer of interests in bank accounts (except where the account is the proceeds of collateral) (§9-104(l))

E. Basic Definitions: The meanings of most of the technical words used in Article 9 will be discussed as the need arises. A few basic terms, however, should be explained at the outset.

  1. Debtor: " 'Debtor' means the person who owes payment or other performance of the obligation secured, whether or not he owns or has rights in the collateral . . . " (§9-105(d), first sentence.) The reason for the last clause in the above sentence is that the person who owes the debt may induce a third person to put up collateral on his behalf. If this happens, the definition of 'debtor' provides that the term means "the owner of the collateral in any provision dealing with the collateral, the obligor in any provision dealing with the obligation, and may include both where the context so requires." The term 'debtor' also includes one who sells accounts or chattel paper, even though this seller does not, strictly speaking, owe a debt to the buyer. However, these sales are covered by Article 9 (see §9-102(1)(b)), and the seller is treated as a 'debtor' for the purpose of the article. §(9-105(1)(d).

  2. Secured party: A secured party is "a lender, seller or other person in whose favor there is a security interest, including a person to whom accounts or chattel paper have been sold." §9-105(1)(m). Both a lender of money (a bank or finance company, for instance) and a seller who gives credit for a portion of the purchase price, are secured parties for Article 9 purposes. (Where a seller gives credit, and takes a security interest in the goods which have been sold, his interest is known as a *"purchase money security interest"* — see §9-107(a) and also the discussion *infra*, p. 22.)

  3. Security interest: A security interest is defined by §1-201(37) as "an interest in personal property or fixtures which secures payment or performance of an obligation." This definition goes on to state that where an agreement for the sale of goods states that the seller *retains title* to the goods until payment is made, this retention establishes *only a security interest*. Thus the *conditional sale*, which reserves title in the vendor until the goods are paid for, is *abolished as a distinct kind of security interest*, and becomes an ordinary Article 9 security interest (a purchase money security interest, since the seller would be the one giving credit.)

   a. Lease as security interest: §1-201(37)'s definition of security interest also discusses the determination of whether a lease is a security interest — this matter will be discussed more fully *infra*, this page.

    b. Limitation on §1-201(37)'s definition: Insofar as §1-201(37)'s definition of 'security interest' implies that *any* interest in personal property or fixtures which secures repayment is a security interest, it has been suggested that "this definition cannot be taken at face value." (W&S, 876). This definition is so broad that *any* distinctive claim that a creditor might have to the assets of his debtor would be an interest securing repayment, and thus a security interest. For example, suppose a debtor agrees with his creditor that he will not grant to any other creditor a security interest in his personal property until he has paid off this particular creditor. Such a "negative pledge" grants an "interest" securing repayment, yet most commentators agree that there is no Article 9 security interest. As Gilmore (1 Gilmore 336) has put it, Article 9 was drafted only to "regulate certain wellknown and institutionalized types of financing transactions."

    4. Collateral: Collateral is "the property subject to a security interest, and includes accounts and chattel paper which have been sold." (§9-105(1)(c)). Collateral for Article 9 purposes thus means not only property which is transferred to the security party's possession, but also any property which remains in the debtor's possession, and which may be seized by the secured party on default.

III. LEASES AS SECURITY INTERESTS

    A. How question arises: Suppose Manufacturer, a producer of printing presses, and Printer, who needs a press, make a deal that is in the form of a lease. The lease states that Printer is to be the lessee of the equipment for a period of five years, that he is to make monthly payments of a certain sum, and that if he falls behind, Manufacturer may repossess the press. Suppose also that the lease provides that at the end of the five year period, Printer may obtain title to the press by paying 10% of the price for which the press sells when new.

    1. Difficulty: In the above example, it might be argued that Manufacturer isn't really "leasing" the press at all, but that it is *selling* it and reserving a security interest. On the other hand, it might be argued that Printer is a true lessee, because he is not building up any equity in the press — at the end of the lease term, he will not own the press. The difficulty of determining whether a lease should be treated as a sale-and-security-interest has led to a great deal of litigation, because much turns on the result in many cases.

    B. Importance of question: While the question of whether a lease is a security interest often has practical importance even if the debtor/lessee does not go bankrupt, the question is even more important in the bankruptcy context. The reason for this will become clearer in the discussion of bankruptcy below; for the moment, the following explanation will suffice:

1. **Trustee's right to invalidate unperfected security interest:** The trustee in bankruptcy, who is a representative of the bankrupt's unsecured creditors, is given certain powers by the Bankruptcy Code. Among these powers is the right to invalidate any security interest which is not "perfected" at the date of bankruptcy. The concept of "perfection" will be discussed more extensively *infra*, p. 21; it relates to certain formalities which must be complied with, usually a *filing* to give public notice of the existence of a security interest.

   a. **Consequence of non-perfection:** The trustee is therefore likely to argue that a particular transaction between a third party and the bankrupt was a security interest that was unperfected. The third party, however, will argue that his interest was not a security interest at all — for example, by saying that it was a *lease*. (The lessor has the right to reclaim the leased property after bankruptcy, unless the trustee elects to continue the lease.) If, on the other hand, the third-party creditor has only a security interest, the automatic stay provisions of the Bankruptcy Code will limit his ability to get the equipment back promptly; see *infra*, p. 128.

      Example: Suppose that in the above example, Manufacturer does not give any public notice of his transaction with Printer. If this transaction is ultimately held to have been a security interest, it will be an *unperfected* security interest. If Printer goes bankrupt, his trustee will argue that the "lease" was really an unperfected security interest, which the trustee can invalidate. Manufacturer will argue that the transaction was a true lease, and that he therefore has the right to reclaim the press.

C. **Treatment of leases in UCC:** The UCC itself gives some guidance as to when a transaction that is cast in the form of a lease is to be treated as creating a security interest. §1-201(37)'s definition of "security interest" states that "unless a lease . . . is intended as security, reservation of title thereunder is not a 'security interest'. . . ."

1. **Significance of option to purchase:** §1-201(37) then goes on to state that although whether a lease is intended as security is to be determined from the facts of each case, two rules of construction are to be observed:

a. **Option to purchase by itself:** "The inclusion of an option to purchase does not of itself make the lease one intended for security;" and

b. **Purchase option with nominal consideration:** "An agreement that upon compliance with the terms of the lease, the lessee shall become or have the option to become the owner of the property for no additional consideration or for a nominal consideration does make the lease one intended for security."

2. **Option for no or nominal consideration:** As subparagraph (b) above states, any time the lessee has an option to buy the property for no or a *"nominal"* consideration, the lease is to be treated as a security interest.

   a. **Meaning of "nominal":** Most courts have held that whether the option price is "nominal" is to be determined by *comparing that price to the market value of the leased property at the time of the option's exercise*.

      Example: At the end of the lease term, the leased property would be worth about $10,000. The lease provides that at the end of the term, the lessee may purchase it for a payment of $1,000. "The best test [for determining "nominalness"] is a comparison of the option price with the market value of the equipment at the time the option is to be exercised." Since the option price was only one-tenth of the actual value, the payment was "nominal," and the lease is therefore a security interest. *Peco, Inc. v. Hartbauer Tool & Dye Co.*, 500 P.2d 708 (Ore. 1972).

   b. **Right to terminate transaction:** At least one court has held that if the lessee has the right to *terminate the transaction* before the purchase option ever arises, the option does *not* make the lease a security interest. *In re Marhoefer Packing Co., Inc.*, 674 F.2d 1139 (7th Cir. 1982). Thus in *Marhoefer*, there were two option-to-purchase clauses: the first provided that at the end of the basic four-year lease term, the lessee could purchase the leased machine for $10,000; the second provided that the lessee could instead renew the lease for an additional four-year term, at the conclusion of which he could purchase the equipment for one dollar. The court held that the presence of the second, one dollar, option did not transform the lease into a security interest, because the lessee could instead terminate the lease after a basic four-year term. §1-201(37)'s automatic rule that the presence of a nominal-cost option makes the lease a security interest applies "only when [the option] necessarily arises upon compliance with the terms of the lease." (By contrast, the $10,000 necessary to purchase the leased machine under the first option was found by the court not to be "nominal" because it amounted to at least 50% of the expected fair market value of the machine at the time for exercise.)

3. **Other relevant factors:** Other facts that courts have considered in determining whether a lease is intended as security include "the *total amount of rent* the lessee is required to pay under the lease, whether the lessee acquires any *equity* in the leased property, the *useful life* of the leased goods, the nature of the lessor's business, and the payment of *taxes*, insurance and other charges normally imposed on ownership." *Marhoefer, supra.*

4. *In re Royer's Bakery:* §1-201(37) was construed in *In re Royer's Bakery*, 4 CCH Inst. Cr. Guide par. 99,274. There, a lease of baking equipment gave the lessee the right to purchase, any time during the term of the lease, the equipment for the list price minus "80% of the aggregate rental payments previously made . . . up to, but not exceeding, the list price of the piece of equipment."

   a. **Holding:** The court held that the above provision in the lease made the lease a security interest by the logic of §1-201(37). "By crediting earlier payments of rent to the purchase price, the lessee is accorded an equity or pecuniary interest in the subject of the lease which he may recover at his option. [In such a case] the parties are deemed as a matter of law to have intended the lease as security. . . ."

5. **Economic Realities test for leases:** Some courts have applied an "economic realities" test in determining whether a particular lease was a security interest. By this test, if at the end of the lease term the only sensible economic course for the lessee is for him to exercise his option to purchase, then the transaction is a security interest, even though the lessee must make a sizeable payment to exercise his purchase option.

   Example: In *In re Washington Processing Co.*, 3 UCC Rep. Serv. 475, the lessee was entitled to become owner of the leased machine for $1,350 at the end of the lease term. Since the fair market value of the machine at that time would be between $7500 and $10,500, the court concluded that the "lessee" had been building up an equity in the machinery, rather than merely making rental payments. The original transaction was therefore held to have been an "installment sale" governed by Article 9, not a "true lease."

   a. **Formula:** The economic realities test has been stated as follows: "If the amount the lessee must pay to exercise his option is roughly equal to the fair market value of the asset at that time, then the transaction is not a secured sale." W&S, 881.

6. **Lack of purchase option not dispositive:** It is not the case that if the lessee has no option to purchase at all, his interest is not a security interest. Prof. Gilmore states the following example: "Assume . . . that a piece of equipment is estimated to have a useful life of 3 years, at the end of which time it will have little or no remaining value. The 'lease' requires the lessee to pay during the three years an amount equivalent to the purchase price (or purchase price less scrap value) and provides that at the end of this term the lessor will retake the goods. On the facts hypothesized, the arrangement should be held to be one 'intended for security,' despite the absence of any option to purchase." Note that this case fails to be a security interest under the economic realities test, since it is not the case that the only sensible course for the lessee is to become the owner at the end of the lease term — the equipment is worth nothing at that point.

7. **Financing statement irrelevant:** One factor that will **not** be relevant to the lease-vs.-secured-transaction issue is the existence of a *financing statement*. §9-408 states that a lessor may use the words "lessor", "lessee", and the like, rather than the words "secured party", "debtor", etc., and that the filing of a financing statement "shall not of itself be a factor in determining whether or not the consignment or lease is intended as security." The section notes that "however, if it is determined for other reasons that the . . . lease is so intended, a security interest of the . . . lessor which attaches to the . . . leased goods is perfected by such filing."

   a. **Utility:** Thus if the lessor fears that the economic aspects of the transaction may lead to its being considered a secured transaction, he can protect himself by filing, without increasing the possibility that the lease will be held to be a secured transaction.

   b. **Not in 1962 Code:** §9-408 is present only in the 1972, not the 1962, version of Article 9.

IV. CONSIGNMENTS AS SECURITY INTERESTS

A. **Consignments generally:** Wholesalers or manufacturers of goods often make their sales "*on consignment*". The essence of a consignment sale is that if the consignee is unable to resell the goods, he may return them, and he does not have to pay for them until he sells them. Where goods have been sold on consignment, and are not sold or paid for by the consignee, does the consignor have the right to reclaim the goods in the face of judgments or liens held by the consignee's creditors, or in the face of the consignee's trustee in bankruptcy?

1. **Consignor must file:** This question is answered in §2-326(3). For all practical purposes, the consignor must *file an Article 9 security interest* in the consigned merchandise, or be held to have an interest inferior to that of the consignee's creditors or trustee in bankruptcy.

FORMAL REQUISITES OF A SECURITY INTEREST

I. GENERAL REQUIREMENTS

A. Requisites for enforceability: Before a security interest may be enforced against either the debtor or against third parties, certain formal requirements must be met. The basic set of requirements is encapsulated under the term *"attachment"*. "Attachment" is synonymous with "enforceable against the debtor". (A security interest which has attached may also be valid against a third party, but in some circumstances the additional requirement of "perfection" must be met for there to be priority over third parties; perfection is discussed beginning *infra*, p. 21.)

1. **Meaning of "attachment":** §9-203 sets forth the requirements for a security interest to be enforceable against the debtor, i.e., for it to "attach". Under §9-203(1), three things must happen:

   a. **Pledge or writing:** First, as a matter of what might be called the Article 9 *"Statute of Frauds"*, the debtor must have *"signed a security agreement which contains a description of the collateral . . . "* §9-203(1)(a).

      i. **Description of land:** Furthermore, if the security interest covers *crops* or *timber*, this signed security agreement must contain a *description of the land*. *Id.*

      ii. **Exception for pledge:** But a critical exception to the requirement of a signed writing occurs when the collateral is in the *possession of the secured party*. That is, where there is a *"pledge"*, no written agreement is necessary.

   b. **Debtor has rights in collateral:** Secondly, the debtor must obtain *rights in the collateral*. The meaning of this requirement is discussed *infra*, p. 18.

   c. **Creditor gives value:** Thirdly, the creditor must *"give value"*. In general, he will do this by advancing money or credit, or by legally binding himself to do so. See *infra*, p. 18.

2. **All three must happen:** Until *all three* of these requirements have been met, the security agreement is of no force against the debtor or against any third party.

   Example: Bank and Debtor sign a Security Agreement, in which Bank is given a security interest in all inventory now or thereafter acquired by Debtor. An officer of Bank orally promises Debtor that Bank will almost certainly make him the loan he desires. Yet until Bank actually makes the loan, or legally binds itself to do so (which may require a writing under local law), the security agreement is not enforceable against Debtor. Nor is it enforceable against third parties; thus if a third party took a security interest in the same inventory, and advanced value, all before Bank made a firm commitment or an advance, that other secured party would have priority if neither security interest was ever perfected. (See §9-312(5)(b), *infra*, p. 75.)

3. **Debtor's signature:** The security agreement, as noted, must be ***signed by the debtor***. §1-201(39) defines "signed" to include "any symbol executed or adopted by a party with present intention to authenticate a writing." Thus anything the debtor puts on the paper will be adequate, so long as there is evidence (perhaps parole evidence) that there was an intent to validate the document.

   a. **Typewritten name:** Thus if an individual or business entity's name is ***typewritten***, this will be sufficient to meet the signature requirement so long as there is some other evidence that authentication of the document was intended. See W&S, p. 913.

   b. **Multiple documents:** Suppose the debtor signs one document, but fails to sign another document that contains, say, the description of the collateral. May the court consider both documents together to find that §9-203's requirements have been met? The cases are unclear on this question. If the secured party can show that all documents were prepared at about the same time, as part of the same transaction, and that the debtor approved of all of them, the court may be willing to consider them all together.

II. USE OF FINANCING STATEMENT AS SECURITY AGREEMENT

A. **Reason question arises:** In most transactions where the debtor takes possession of the collateral, the secured party must file a ***financing statement*** in the public records in order to have priority over certain important classes of persons. (§§9-302; 9-303(1)). (This requirement will be discussed extensively *infra* at p. 26.) In such cases, the secured party is often diligent enough to file such a statement, containing the debtor's signature, but he neglects to execute a separate document entitled "security agreement". The question thus arises in later litigation whether the financing statement itself qualifies as a security agreement within the meaning of §9-203(1)(a). If it does, then the secured party may enforce his security interest against the debtor and against certain third persons; if not, he has no rights against anybody according to §9-203(1)(a).

B. Position of the courts: Apparently no court has held that a standard financing statement, with no additional language, constitutes a valid security agreement. See W&S, p. 906. Many of the decisions have relied on the theory that specific "words of grant" establishing a security interest are necessary.

    1. *American Card* **case:** Thus a financing statement was held not to constitute a security agreement in *American Card Co. v. H.M.H. Co.*, 196 A. 2d 150 (1963).

        a. Secured party's argument: The secured party in *American Card*, in arguing that the financing statement it had filed satisfied the requirement of a security agreement, cited §9-402(1). That section, after stating the requirements for a financing statement (under the present code, signature by the debtor, address of the secured party, mailing address of the debtor, and a description of the collateral) states that "a copy of the security agreement is sufficient as a financing statement if it contains the above information and is signed by the debtor.

        b. Holding: The *American Card* court acknowledged that the last clause of §9-402(1) does mean that it is possible for a financing statement and a security agreement to be one and the same document. However, the court continued, the requirement of a security agreement is not satisfied unless the financing statement contains the debtor's ***grant of a security interest*** to the secured party. "The financing statement which the claimants filed clearly fails to qualify also as a security agreement because nowhere in the form is there any evidence of an agreement by the debtor to grant the claimants a security interest.

        c. Criticism of *American Card***:** The holding in *American Card* has been widely criticized by the commentators (though no court has reached a directly contrary result). Gilmore states (1 Gilmore 348) that the financing statement in *American Card* contained sufficient evidence of the parties' intention to create a security interest. He argues that "no doubt the court would have upheld the security interest if the debtor had signed two pieces of paper instead of one. The §9-402 provision that a short financing statement may be filed instead of the full security agreement was designed to simplify the operation. The [*American Card*] court gives it an effect reminiscent of the worst formal requisites holding under the nineteenth century chattel mortgage acts.

      i. Meaning of "agreement": Criticism of the decision in *American Card* is buttressed by §1-201(3)'s definition of "agreement" — " 'agreement' means the bargain of the parties in fact as found in their language or by implication from other circumstances including course of dealing or usage of trade or course of performance as provided in this Act." In other words, the bargain of the parties may be ascertained by implication from the circumstances surrounding their negotiation or from their usual manner of doing business. The *American Card* court's insistence that unless the financing statement expressly grants a security interest, there is no security agreement, would therefore seem to fly in the face of §1-201(3)'s definition of "agreement".

    d. Pre-filing: Since the court's decision was founded upon the lack of a specific grant by the debtor of a security interest, one wonders what else the debtor could have meant to do by signing the financing statement other than to grant a security interest. However, §9-402(1) provides that "A financing statement may be filed before a security agreement is made or a security interest otherwise attaches." In other words, a financing statement may be "pre-filed", so that when a security interest does come into existence, it is immediately perfected. Thus the debtor might sign a financing statement in order to allow such pre-filing, without his signature itself constituting a grant of a security interest. (Perhaps the court should have looked at whether the parties conducted further negotiations after the filing, which would have indicated a pre-filing rather than a grant of security.)

2. Financing statement with extra language sufficient: But although a standard "naked" financing statement has never been found sufficient to constitute a security agreement, *additional language* inserted into the financing statement may be enough to validate it as an agreement.

    a. *Evans* **case:** Thus in *Evans v. Everett*, 183 S.E.2d 109 (N.C. 1971), the financing statement provided that it "covers the following types of collateral . . . same *securing* note for advanced money to produce crops for the year 1969." (Emphasis added.) The parties had also executed a note which stated that it was secured by the financing statement. The court observed that no "magic words" creating a security interest are required, and that there must merely be language which "leads to the logical conclusion that it was the intention of the parties that a security interest be created." The financing statement's reference to the fact that the crops were security for the note made it quite clear that there was an intent to create a security interest in those crops; therefore, the requirement of a security agreement was held to have been met by the financing statement.

3. **Use of miscellaneous signed writings as security agreement:** Similarly, some courts, interested in enforcing the actual intent of the parties, have held that signed writings other than a formal security agreement can in effect be "pasted together" to satisfy the requirements of §9-203(1)(a). For instance, subsequent *correspondence* between the parties may show that they believe a security interest was created, and the court may find this sufficient to meet §9-203(1)(a)'s requirement of a signed security agreement.

> **Example:** Debtor borrows funds from Z&J and executes a promissory note providing that the loan is secured by "security interests in a certain Security Agreement to be delivered by [Debtor] to Z&J with this Promissory Note covering [certain machinery and equipment]." No formal security agreement is in fact executed by the parties. Z&J files a financing statement containing a detailed list of the machinery and equipment identified by the note as collateral. After the loan is made, the parties exchange a series of letters which refer to the substitution or impairment of Z&J's collateral.
>
> *Held*, the note, financing statement and letters, when considered together, satisfy the requirements of §9-203(1)(a). The financing statement meets the basic requirement that there be a writing, signed by the debtor, describing the collateral. The promissory note provides an expression of future intent to create a security interest, and the letters demonstrate that the parties believed a security interest had been created. *In re Bollinger*, 614 F.2d 924 (3rd Cir. 1980).

III. REQUIREMENT THAT COLLATERAL BE DESCRIBED

A. **General requirement:** §9-203(1) provides that, unless the collateral is in the possession of the secured party, the debtor must have signed a security agreement "which contains a description of the collateral . . . "

1. **Specificity not required:** §9-110 states, however, that "for the purposes of this Article, any description of personal property or real estate is sufficient whether or not it is specific if it *reasonably identifies* what is described."

B. **Courts' approach:** Most courts have been reasonably liberal in interpreting the requirement that the collateral be described in the security agreement. Courts have taken to heart §9-110's statement that *"reasonable identification"* is all that is required.

1. **Extrinsic evidence:** Generally, if the secured party can show by *extrinsic* evidence (i.e., evidence outside the security agreement) what particular items of collateral were intended to be covered, he will prevail even though the security agreement itself may be somewhat vague. Thus in *U.S. v. Midstate Sales*, 336 F. Supp. 1099 (D. Neb. 1971), the security agreement gave an interest in "46 cattle", although the debtor was a rancher with 800 cattle. The court held that the description was adequate, but that the secured creditor bore the burden of showing by external evidence which forty-six head of cattle were intended to be covered, in order to obtain priority over another secured party.

2. **Serial number error:** Where the collateral consists of machinery which is described by *serial number*, the courts have usually held that minor errors in the serial number are not fatal. Again, the test is whether, notwithstanding the serial number error, the collateral can be reasonably clearly identified at the time of the litigation.

3. **Misleading of other creditors:** However, the court may well hold the description inadequate if there is evidence that it actually or potentially *misled* other creditors about what was covered.

   > **Example:** The security agreement gives Creditor a security interest in all of the Debtor's accounts receivable, inventory, fixtures, machinery, equipment and tools. In addition to this broad "omnibus" clause, there is a listing of certain individual items, including a truck. After Debtor goes bankrupt, Creditor asserts that the omnibus clause covered two automobiles owned by Debtor. *Held*, the automobiles were not adequately described in the agreement. A creditor examining the document would, after seeing the reference to the truck, assume that no other vehicles were covered notwithstanding the omnibus clause. Because of this potential misleading of creditors, the description must be held inadequate, and the cars are not covered. *In re Laminated Veneers Co., Inc.*, 471 F.2d 1124 (2d Cir. 1973).

   > **Note:** Observe that in *Laminated Veneers*, there was no actual creditor who was misled by an examination of the security agreement. The court nonetheless found that the *potential* for misleading creditors was sufficient to render the description inadequate. This seems unduly strict, and White and Summers (at p. 904) argue that only *actual* reliance by other creditors, not potential reliance, should be considered in determining the adequacy of a description, a signature, or any of the other formal requirements of §9-203.

4. **After-acquired property clauses:** One area in which the courts are particularly likely to be strict is in the context of *after-acquired property* clauses. Such clauses provide that property subsequently acquired by the debtor shall be covered by the security agreement. (See *infra*, p. 18). Because of the possible abuses of such "dragnet" clauses, by which every item that the debtor ever acquires will be covered, courts have required reasonably precise descriptions.

> **Example:** Debtor, a grain dealer, buys grain from farmers and resells it to large grain concerns, such as D (Cargill, a large grain company). In order to get financing from Bank, Debtor signs a security agreement with Bank under which Debtor gives Bank as security "all monies now due or to become due under certain Grain Contracts held in your Warehouse." Bank gives D notice of this assignment, and tells it to send the contract payments to Bank, not to Debtor. On certain contracts that come into existence *after* Debtor has given the security interest to Bank, D pays Debtor directly instead of paying Bank. After Debtor defaults on its payments to Bank, Bank sues D for the amounts paid by D to Debtor on the post-security-interest contracts.
>
> *Held*, for D. There was a valid security interest between Debtor and Bank covering payments due (or to become due) to Debtor under contracts *already existing* at the time the security interest was created. But the security interest did not mention "after-acquired property," and nothing in the parties' course of dealings showed an intent to cover such after-acquired property. Therefore, there was no security interest in payments due under any contract that came into existence after the Bank-Debtor security interest was created, so D does not have to pay anything to Bank under these contracts. *Idaho Bank & Trust Co. v. Cargill, Inc.*, 665 P.2d 1093 (Idaho 1983).
>
> **Note:** The court in *Idaho Bank & Trust* also held that *"future advances"* by Bank to Debtor were not covered by the security agreement. That is, subsequent loans made by Bank to Debtor, after creation of the security agreement, were not covered because the agreement did not expressly state that such future advances would be covered. See pp. 109-13 *infra*, for further discussion of future advances.

a. **No after-acquired property interest in consumer goods:** Digressing a moment, observe that the Code has another way of protecting against unduly onerous after-acquired property clauses. Under §9-204(4)(b), no after-acquired property interest is allowed in *consumer goods* unless the consumer acquires these goods within ten days of the time the secured party makes his loan. (An exception occurs in the case of so-called "accessions", or "attachments" to covered collateral, under §9-314.)

IV. OTHER REQUIREMENTS FOR ENFORCEABILITY

A. Value given and rights received: In addition to a signed agreement in the proper form, two other things must happen before the security agreement is enforceable against the debtor or any third parties: (1) *value* must be given by the secured party; and (2) the debtor must have received *rights* in the collateral. Each of these is discussed separately below.

B. Giving of value: The security interest cannot become enforceable until the secured party *"gives value"*. §9-203(1)(b). §1-201(44) states that a person gives "value" for rights if he acquires them in certain enumerated ways. Among the ways a secured party gives value in return for a security interest are:

1. By *committing himself* (legally binding himself) to *extend credit*;

2. By taking a security interest to satisfy a *pre-existing claim*;

3. "in return for any consideration sufficient to support a simple contract."

> **Example:** Secured Party and Debtor sit down to discuss the granting to Secured Party of a security interest. Even if Debtor signs a security agreement, these discussions do not constitute the giving of value by Secured Party, so the security agreement cannot be effective yet. But if Secured Party legally binds himself to make a loan to Debtor, or to sell Debtor goods on credit, he has "given value." Or, if Debtor already owed money to Secured Party, and Secured Party is now taking a security interest to secure repayment of the debt, this is the giving of value by Secured Party. Finally, if the state in which the deal is made follows the "peppercorn" theory of consideration, by which the payment of purely nominal consideration by one contracting party to another is sufficient consideration, then by paying Debtor one dollar for his security interest, Secured Party has met the "giving value" requirement.

C. Debtor's rights in the collateral: The final requirement for enforceability is that the Debtor must have *rights in the collateral*. §9-203(1)(c). The Code does not, however, state explicitly the rules for determining when the Debtor has rights in the collateral. (§9-204(2) of the 1962 Code, which did set forth rules for certain types of collateral, has been dropped from the present Code.)

1. **After-acquired property:** §9-204(1) validates the *after-acquired property* clause. Since such a clause applies the security interest to property not yet acquired by the debtor, it is hard to see how the security interest can be enforceable with respect to this after-acquired property until the debtor actually acquires rights in it.

   a. **Entity theory:** However, suppose that the after-acquired property clause covers inventory or accounts receivable, and that at the time the agreement is signed the debtor has at least some inventory and/or some accounts. (Such a security interest in after-acquired inventory and accounts is often called a "floating lien", discussed further *infra*, p. 141.) A number of courts have held that the secured party's security interest is in the "mass" or "entity" of accounts receivable or inventory. Therefore, these courts hold, the security interest becomes enforceable against this category of collateral as an entity; other items in the same class, though not yet acquired, are covered from the date the interest in the original goods becomes enforceable. This is the so-called *"entity theory"*.

      Example: Bank and Auto Dealer sign a security agreement covering all presently-owned and after-acquired inventory of Dealer, on February 1. On that date, Dealer holds a number of cars in inventory. In courts following the "entity theory", this security agreement becomes immediately binding against Dealer and third parties even though the individual items (the cars) making up Dealer's inventory will constantly be changing.

   b. **Question not critical:** Even if the court does not accept the "entity" theory or its equivalent, the same result with respect to priorities usually ensues. The only time the question of exactly when the agreement became enforceable is important is in calculating which of several competing interests has priority. Yet the rules of priority (discussed *infra*, p. 74) generally make it irrelevant whether the after-acquired property is covered from the date of the original agreement or only from the date of acquisition. (But the issue does become significant in certain bankruptcy problems; see *infra*, p. 143.)

2. **Buyer of goods:** A *buyer of goods* will be deemed to have rights in them once he takes possession; this is true (according to most courts) even if the goods are paid for with a *check* which *bounces*. See W&S, p. 917. (Therefore, the buyer's secured party with an after-acquired property interest will take prior to the seller. But the seller may have a right of reclamation under §2-702, which may or may not be superior to the right of the secured party; see the discussion of the reclamation right in the bankruptcy context *infra*, p.

155.)

a. Prior to delivery: There are some situations where the debtor may even have rights in collateral which he has purchased, but which has *not yet been delivered*.

Example: §2-501(1)(b) provides that the buyer of goods obtains a "special property and an insurable interest in goods . . . when goods are shipped, marked or otherwise designated by the seller as goods to which the contract refers." Thus a debtor entitled to receive shipment of goods has "rights" in those goods even before he receives them (in fact, even before they have left the seller's hands) if the seller has marked or identified the particular goods he will send (as by packing or labeling them.)

b. Mere possession not enough: But *mere possession* of the goods by the debtor will probably not be sufficient to constitute "rights" in them. See, e.g., *Cain v. Country Club Delicatessen of Saybrook, Inc.*, 203 A.2d 441 (Conn. Super. Ct., 1964), where the collateral was restaurant equipment, possession of which had been given to the debtor several weeks before any written conditional sales contract for the equipment was signed. In the absence of evidence about the arrangements whereby the debtor had this possession, the court refused to find that the debtor had rights in the collateral. Therefore, the security interest was not deemed to have attached until the contract was signed.

PERFECTION

I. PERFECTION GENERALLY

A. Meaning of perfection: If the formal requirements discussed in the previous chapters have been met, a security interest is valid and enforceable against the debtor. The secured party is, however, interested in being able to assert his rights even as against certain third parties. For example, he is interested in having priority against a person who becomes a lien creditor of the debtor (e.g., the holder of a judgment against the debtor who has levied on the debtor's property covered by the security agreement) after the security interest has attached. Or he may be interested in having priority over another person with a security interest in the same collateral. In order to gain priority over these third persons, the secured party must generally *perfect* his security interest.

    1. Term of art: "Perfection" is a term of art as it is used in Article 9. In some situations, a security interest is perfected as soon as it attaches. In other cases, it is temporarily perfected for 21 days. In still another class of cases, it is perfected for as long as the secured party keeps possession of the collateral. In the vast majority of cases, however, the secured party must give *public notice* by filing a *financing statement*.

II. VARIOUS MEANS OF PERFECTION

A. Transactions excluded from filing requirement: Most security interests can be perfected only through the filing of a financing statement. However, §9-302(1) excludes several categories of security interests from the filing requirement. Among the more important exceptions to the filing requirement are:

    1. a security interest in property in the *possession of the secured party;*

    2. a *purchase money security interest in consumer goods* (except registered motor vehicles);

    3. an assignment of accounts which does *not* alone or in conjunction with other assignments to the same assignee *transfer a significant part* of the outstanding accounts of the assignor;

    4. a security interest *temporarily perfected* in *instruments* or *documents* under §9-304;

    5. a security interest in *proceeds*, for a 10 day period, if the security interest in the original collateral was perfected. (See §9-306(3).

B. Purchase money interests in consumer goods: In order to determine whether the above exceptions apply, one must be able to determine whether the security interest is, for example, in consumer goods, or whether it is instead in non-consumer goods. A similar problem is posed with respect to "instruments" and "documents." The categories of "instruments", "documents", "accounts", and "contract rights" will be considered *infra*, p. 40. Here, we will consider the definitions relevant to §9-302(1)(d), that is, "purchase money security interest" and "consumer goods".

1. **Purchase money security interest:** Two distinct classes of persons can take a *purchase money security interest* in goods. These two categories of secured parties are set forth in §9-107:

    a. **Seller:** A security interest "taken or retained by the *seller* of the collateral to secure all or part of its price" is a purchase money security interest (§9-107(a)). In other words, a *seller who sells on credit* has a purchase money interest if he has a security interest at all.

    b. **Lender:** One who lends money to the debtor in order to *enable the latter to buy goods* obtains a purchase money interest in the goods, if the loan is *in fact used* to buy the goods.

2. **Consumer goods:** §9-109 divides the category of "goods" into four sub-classes: "consumer goods", "equipment", "farm products", and "inventory". These groups are mutually exclusive — "the same property cannot at the same time and as to the same person be both equipment and inventory, for example." (Comment 2 to §9-109).

    a. **Definition of "consumer goods":** §9-109(1) defines *"consumer goods"* as follows: "Goods are 'consumer goods' if they are used or bought for use primarily for *personal*, *family* or *household* purposes." Observe that this definition depends upon the use to which the goods are put by the debtor. " . . . a radio is inventory in the hands of a dealer and consumer goods in the hands of a householder." (Comment 2, §9-109.)

    b. **Definition of "inventory":** *"Inventory"* is goods that are held "for sale or lease", or "to be furnished under contracts of service", or that are "raw materials, work in progress or materials used or consumed in a business." (§9-109(4)).

    c. **Definition of "equipment":** "Equipment," broadly speaking, is *any goods held for use in business* that do not fall within the definition of *"inventory"* or *"farm products"* (defined in §9-109(3) to include crops, livestock, and the like.) See §9-109(2). Machinery used in a factory, for instance, is equipment.

3. **Perfection of purchase money interest:** A purchase money security interest in consumer goods is ***automatically perfected*** as soon as the security interest attaches. Thus neither filing, nor any other act, is necessary for perfection. §9-302(1)(d).

> **Example:** Merchant sells Consumer a washing machine on credit. Merchant's interest is a purchase money security interest, since he is a seller taking his interest to secure the purchase price. The washing machine is "consumer goods" since it is bought for use primarily for personal or household purposes. By §9-302(1)(d), therefore, no filing is required for perfection. §9-303(1) provides that "a security interest is perfected when it has attached and when all of the applicable steps required for perfection have been taken." Thus, the interest is perfected as soon as (1) Consumer has signed a valid security agreement; (2) Consumer has rights in the collateral; (3) there is agreement that the interest attach; and (4) Merchant gives value. This will probably all happen when Consumer signs a contract giving her the right to have the machine delivered and providing for installment payments.

a. **Written interest:** Keep in mind that the fact that ***attachment*** is a pre-requisite to perfection means that in the ordinary purchase money security interest situation, there must be a written security interest, signed by the debtor.

> **Example:** Buyer buys a stove from Dealer for use in her home. Dealer has no more conditional sales contract forms, but he shows Buyer a contract signed by a previous customer, Mrs. Brown. Buyer and Dealer make an oral agreement that they will adhere to the terms of the Brown contract, and Buyer makes a $50 down payment, as was required by the Brown contract. Buyer then takes the stove home with her.
>
> Dealer's security interest is not perfected (or even attached). Neither attachment nor perfection can occur unless there is a valid written security agreement, signed by Buyer. See §9-203(1)(a).
>
> As an interesting sidelight, under the old version of Article 9, the security interest was probably ***attached***, and ***perfected***, even though it was not enforceable against the debtor or anyone else! The anomaly of having an interest that was attached and even perfected, yet not enforceable, was corrected by redrafting in the 1972 Code, so that the concepts of enforceability and attachment are now synonymous. Under the present version of §9-203, a security interest created by oral agreement can attach and be enforced only where the secured party has ***possession*** of the collateral (i.e., a pledge); this did not happen on the facts of this Example.

C. Perfection by possession: If the collateral, no matter what kind, is in the possession of the secured party, the security interest is perfected without the filing of a financing statement. (§9-302(1)(a)).

> **Example:** Gambler pawns his watch to Pawnbroker for $10. He receives a pledge ticket which has a receipt and Pawnbroker's name and address on it, but no other writing. He now wants to get his watch back without paying for it.
>
> Pawnbroker has an enforceable, perfected, security agreement; this situation is an example of the formal requirements which can be satisfied by the secured party's mere possession of the collateral. Under §9-203(1)(a), no written security agreement is necessary if the secured party has possession of the collateral. §9-305 allows a security interest in goods to be perfected by the secured party's taking possession of the collateral. (Note that, under §9-305, a security interest perfected by possession continues perfected "only so long as possession is retained . . .", unless another means, generally filing, is used to perfect.)

1. **What can be possessed:** There are, however, a few kinds of collateral which are not considered "possessable" by Article 9. Thus *accounts* and *general intangibles* cannot be perfected by possession. (All other kinds of collateral fit into the list in the first sentence of §9-305.) The reason these kinds of collateral are excluded is that they are "property not ordinarily represented by any writing whose delivery operates to transfer the claim." (Comment 1 to §9-305.)

   a. **Rationale for perfection by possession:** The reason for this exclusion is clear when one considers the general rationale for allowing perfection by possession. The theory is that since the purpose of perfection is to put third parties on notice that the secured party claims a security interest, possession by the secured party will do this. A third person who contemplates making a loan to the debtor against goods not in the debtor's possession will be placed on notice that the debtor may not have full unencumbered rights in the collateral. The same is true with respect to a loan against stocks (which are "instruments" under §9-105(1)(g)) — if the debtor has given possession of these stocks as a pledge to a secured party, a third person will realize that the debtor may no longer have full rights in these stocks, and will make further inquiries. In the case of accounts and general intangibles, the same is not true. One cannot really "possess" an account — there is no piece of paper which embodies the account. Thus, "Even if the creditor collects ledger cards, journals, computer print-outs, sales slips and any other items believed to represent receivables, he will not by those acts perfect a security interest in accounts . . . One creditor might seize ledger cards, another a computer print-out and a third the sales slips. When there is such doubt in the business world about what if anything represents a property interest, possession is not a reliable method of perfection." W&S, 934.

2. **Duties of party in possession:** The secured party, once he takes possession of the collateral, bears certain obligations to the debtor. Under §9-207(1), "A secured party must use ***reasonable care*** in the custody and preservation of collateral in his possession. (Emphasis added.) That section goes on to state that in the case of an instrument or chattel paper. "reasonable care includes taking necessary steps to preserve rights against prior parties unless otherwise agreed."

> **Example:** P borrows money from D Bank to purchase some Boeing debentures. The debentures are convertible into common stock of Boeing. D Bank receives a pledge of the debentures as security for repayment of the loan. The next year, Boeing publishes a notice that the debentures are being redeemed, and that after a certain date the right to convert the debentures into common stock will terminate. P does not receive written notice of this redemption, since the debentures are in bearer form. D Bank's employees fail to notify P of the redemption, or to present the debentures for redemption. The termination date passes, and because the debentures have not been converted, they lose two-thirds of their value.
>
> *Held*, D violated its §9-207(1) duty to take "necessary steps to preserve rights against prior parties. . . ." Therefore, it must make up the loss to P. *Traverse v. Liberty Bank & Trust Co.*, 5 UCC Rep. Serv. 535 (Mass. Super. Ct. 1967).

a. **Limits on duty:** However, §9-207(2) sets certain limits upon the secured party's responsibilities. For instance, the risk of ***accidental loss or damage*** is on the debtor, not the secured party, to the extent of any deficiency in insurance coverage. §9-207(2)(b). Also, the secured party may ***repledge*** the collateral on terms which do not impair the debtor's right to redeem it (§9-207(2)(e), and he may ***commingle*** the collateral with other property provided that the collateral is of a "fungible" nature (e.g., grain). (§9-207(2)(d).)

B. **Instruments perfectible only by possession:** A security interest in ***instruments*** (other than instruments which are part of chattel paper — see the discussion of "chattel paper" *infra*, p. 47) can be perfected ***only*** by possession, except for the possibility of temporary perfection under §9-304(4) and (5). This is discussed further *infra* at p. 46.

1. **What constitutes possession:** It is not always clear whether the secured party has in fact "possessed" the collateral. Difficulties arise when the secured party claims that possession by a "bailee" constituted perfection.

   a. **Debtor never accepted as bailee:** Some secured parties have claimed that the debtor himself was a bailee for the secured party, and therefore that the security interest was perfected by possession. However, this argument has been universally rejected. Comment 2 to §9-305 states that "possession may be by the secured party himself or by an agent on his behalf; it is of course clear, however, that the debtor or a person controlled by him cannot qualify as such an agent for the secured party.

2. *Chapman* **case:** Since a security interest in an instrument can be perfected only through possession, problems arise where the debtor seeks to give two security interests in the same instrument. Unless one of the secured parties can be said to "hold" for the other, then the latter's security interest will not be perfected. This problem was discussed in *In re Chapman*, 5 UCC Rep. Serv. 649 (Ref. Bnkrpcy W.D.Mich. 1968). The court held that one secured party could indeed be said to have "held" for another so that both security interests in the instrument were perfected.

III. PERFECTION BY FILING

A. **Purpose of filing:** Article 9 adopts a system of *"notice filing."* The theory behind "notice filing" is that something should be on public file simply to *alert credit searchers* that a certain security agreement may exist. Then, if the credit searcher is interested, he can contact one of the parties to determine the precise details of the arrangement. The filing merely puts the searcher on notice and tells him where to look for more information.

B. **Interests for which filing required:** Except for certain interests listed in §9-302(1) and discussed above, a security interest can *only* be perfected by *filing a financing statement*.

   1. **Certificate of title act:** Some states have statutes providing for the central filing of security interests in motor vehicles, or for the notation on a certificate of title of a security interest in a vehicle. Where such a state statute exists, §9-302(3)(b) requires that the state non-UCC statute generally be complied with, rather than the UCC filing requirement. This subject will be discussed further at p. 46.

C. **Where to file:** Because there was much dispute about whether a filing system should be state-wide or county-wide, the Code draftsmen have presented three alternative provisions governing the place of filing of a financing statement. These three alternative forms of §9-401(1) differ substantially, and a state enacting the UCC may choose whichever of the three it wishes.

1. **First Alternative:** Under Alternative One, only certain interests which are identified with real estate must be locally filed, and all other items are filed in a single state-wide repository. These real-estate-like interests are: (1) interests in *fixtures* (discussed *infra*, p. 117); (2) interests in *timber* to be cut; (3) interests in *minerals*, including oil and gas; and (4) interests in *accounts* arising from the sale of minerals, including oil and gas, at the wellhead or mine-head. As to all of these interests, they are to be filed in the office where a *mortgage on the real estate* involved would be recorded; this will generally mean the *county* where the land lies. Everything else is filed in the central state office (usually the Secretary of State's office.)

2. **Second Alternative:** Alternative Two establishes the same local-filing rules for real-estate-related interests as does Alternative One. In addition, it provides for local filing (usually county-wide) for security interests in: (1) *farm*-related collateral (farming equipment, farm products, accounts arising from the sale of farm products by a farmer, *crops*, etc.); and (2) *consumer goods*. All of these locally-filed items are to be filed in the *county* of the debtor's residence, except that crops are to be filed in the county where the land is located. All other items are to be filed in the statewide central office.

3. **Third Alternative:** Alternative Three treats farm collateral, consumer goods, crops, minerals and fixtures the same as they are treated in the second alternative. In all other cases, however, if the debtor has a "place of business" in only one county, the creditor must file in *two* places: *in that county* and *also with the Secretary of State*. Similarly, in all these additional cases, if the debtor has no place of business in the state, but resides in the state (as in the case of a resident consumer) there must be filing in the county of the debtor's residence as well as with the Secretary of State. In the case of a debtor with places of business in more than one county, only filing with the Secretary of State is required.

   a. **Place of business:** The courts have had difficulty in determining whether a debtor has a place of business in more than one county. White & Summers suggest that the court should use the *"notoriety"* test, for which the determining factor is "to what extent do creditors and others know that the debtor in fact was doing business at the place in question." W&S, 946-7. A "secret" place of business will thus be irrelevant to the where-to-file issue.

4. **Rationale:** All three alternatives attempt to articulate a difference between transactions that are of essentially local concern, and those that are of state-wide interest. Thus all three alternatives provide for a local filing in the case of real-estate-related interests, such as minerals and fixtures, on the theory that lending in these areas is primarily of local concern, and that other creditors will know how to search the records of the locality (usually the county) where the relevant land lies. Similarly, Alternatives Two and Three reflect the primarily local, not state-wide, scope of farm-related and consumer-goods lending. The principal advantage of *state-wide* lending is that it makes the task of record-searching by large creditors and lenders, with offices in many counties and states, much simpler and therefore much less expensive.

   a. **Most states take Alternative Two:** Alternative Two is the most popular. Twenty-six states have enacted it, compared with twelve for Alternative Three and seven for Alternative One. W&S, p. 942.

5. **Classification of collateral:** The second and third alternative versions of §9-401(1) require the filer to determine whether his collateral is "consumer goods", "farm goods", or something else. While the meaning of "consumer goods" has been discussed *supra*, p. 24, here we address one further problem, which also arises in determining whether collateral is *"farm equipment"* (a subcategory of "equipment"). The definitions of both "consumer goods" and "equipment" in §9-109 include goods which are "used or bought for use" for either consumer or business purposes. The problem is whether it is the debtor's *intended use*, at the time he buys ("bought for use") or his *actual use* ("used") that controls if the two are in conflict. White & Summers advise the court to hold "that the stated intention of the debtor at the time of the loan or purchase governs the filing, even though his actual use differs from his stated intention." W&S, 945.

   a. **"Used in farming operations":** Even after one has decided that certain collateral is "equipment", it may be necessary to determine whether it is furthermore "equipment used in farming operations." For under Alternatives Two and three of §9-401(1), such farming equipment is to be filed against locally, not in the state-wide manner in which other equipment is to be filed against. At least one court has held that if the equipment is *suitable only for use in farming*, it meets the requirements of §9-401(1) (and must therefore be filed against locally), *even if the debtor himself is not a farmer*, and leases the equipment out to others. See *Sequoia Machinery, Inc. v.*

Jarrett, 410 F.2d 1116 (9th Cir. 1969).

6. **Filing made in wrong place:** If a secured party files in the *wrong location*, he is sometimes held to have an unperfected security interest. In other situations, however, he may obtain perfected status in spite of his incorrect filing. §9-401(2) provides that "a filing which is made in good faith in an improper place or not in all the places required by this section" is (1) "nevertheless *effective* with regard to any collateral as to which the filing *complied* with the requirements of this Article"; and is also (2) "effective with regard to collateral covered by the financing statement against any person who has *knowledge* of the contents of such a financing statement."

    a. **Collateral correctly covered:** Provision (1) above is just common sense; where a financing statement attempts to cover more than one kind of collateral (e.g. consumer goods and non-farm equipment) and the filing statement is filed in the correct office with respect to one of the two kinds of collateral, that collateral is covered even though the other class of collateral is not.

    b. **Knowledge of the contents of statement:** Provision (2) above makes a filing valid against a person who has *"knowledge of the contents"* of the incorrectly filed statement. This provision has caused great confusion in the courts — it has not been clear whether the financing statement is valid only against searchers who have actually seen the incorrect statement, or against all third parties who knew about the security interest, or against third parties who both knew about the security interest and knew that there was a financing statement on file somewhere, or against a class of persons defined in some other way.

      i. **Arguments favoring narrow construction:** In favor of a narrow interpretation of §9-401(2), it may be argued that "knowledge" is defined in §1-201(25) as follows: "A person 'knows' or has 'knowledge' of a fact when he has *actual knowledge* of it." (Emphasis added.) The person who merely should have known of the contents of the financing statement, or who did in fact strongly suspect those contents even though he never saw them with his own eyes, does not seem to fit within this requirement of actual knowledge. Also, the more inquiry into the precise mental state of the other creditor required, the weaker becomes the "pure race" nature of the basic Article 9 priority section, §9-312(5). W&S, p. 950.

ii. **Arguments favoring liberal interpretation:** But arguments may also be made favoring a liberal interpretation (from the perspective of the incorrectly-filing secured party). §1-102(1) states that the UCC shall be "liberally construed and applied to promote its underlying purposes and policies." Also, no lawyer or secured party would ever intentionally rely on §9-401(2) in deciding to make what he knows to be an incorrect or dubious filing; therefore, a very narrow interpretation of that clause will not particularly promote the accuracy of filing in general. W&S, p. 951.

iii. **White and Summers split:** White and Summers are themselves unable to come to agreement about where the line should be drawn; one favors the "narrow" interpretation, the other the "liberal" one. See W&S, pp. 950-51.

D. Duration of financing statement: Once a financing statement has been filed to perfect a security interest, that perfection does not last forever. §9-403(2) provides that a financing statement ceases to be effective *five years* after the filing. Once the statement lapses, the security interest becomes unperfected.

1. **Continuation statement:** This time period may be extended, however, by filing a *"continuation statement"* signed by the secured party; such a statement extends the financing statement for five years past the date on which the original statement would have lapsed. §9-403(3)). The continuation must be filed during the time that the original financing statement is still effective, but not earlier than 6 months before the original expiration date. §9-403(2) and (3). If the original statement is allowed to lapse, a new ordinary financing statement would have to be filed, and priority would date only from the filing of the new statement. (§9-303(2) makes an interest which has been perfected by two different methods "continuously perfected" only if the second act of perfection occurred while the first one was still in force.)

   a. **Use of new financing statement as continuation statement:** Suppose the secured party, instead of filing a "continuation statement," files a *second financing statement*. This second financing statement will generally *not* serve the function of a continuation statement, i.e., it will not preserve the effectiveness of the original financing statement.

   Example: On March 25, 1976, Finance Co. files a financing statement covering the proceeds of Debtor's crops on an Ohio farm. On March 17, 1981, Finance Co. files a second financing statement listing the same collateral as that covered by the first filing; this second statement makes no reference to the first. No continuation statement is filed. On May 3,

1982, FHA (a federal lending agency) files a financing statement listing the same collateral covered by Finance Co.'s filings.

Held, FHA has priority with respect to the proceeds of the sale of crops from the farm. Finance Co.'s security interest in the farm became unperfected upon the expiration of its first financing statement on March 25, 1981 (five years after the original filing). The filing of a second financing statement did not preserve Finance Co.'s priority, since the document did not include the elements required for a continuation statement by §9-403(3) (it must be signed by the secured party, identify the original statement by file number, and state that the original statement is still effective). *In re Hays*, 47 B.R. 546 (B.Ct.N.D.Ohio 1985).

2. **Consequences of lapse:** If a security interest becomes unperfected due to the lapse of the financing statement, what are the lapsed party's rights against another secured party who filed his interest while the first (now-lapsed) party's filing was still effective? §9-312(5)(a) gives priority to the first secured party to file if both interests are perfected by filing. (*Infra*, p. 76.) Does the second-to-file party continue to be subordinated even after the first party becomes unperfected through the lapse of the latter's financing statement?

   a. **Lapsed filer loses:** §9-403(2) explicitly provides that "If the security interest becomes unperfected upon lapse, it is deemed to have been ***unperfected*** as against a person who became a purchaser or lien creditor ***before lapse.***" (Emphasis added.) Under §1-201(32) and (33), the term "purchaser" includes a secured party. Therefore, the second-to-file party takes priority over the first-to-file (and now lapsed) party. (But it is not clear that this result follows under the 1962 Code, since the sentence just quoted from §9-403(2) was added in 1972.)

3. **Termination statement:** Once the five-year period passes, §9-403(3) permits the officer in charge of the public files to ***remove*** the financing statement, provided that no continuation statement has been filed. But if the debt is paid off before this, is there any way for the debtor to get the record cleared? Under §9-404, the debtor has the right to require the secured party to file a ***termination statement*** once the debt has been satisfied. In the case of a security interest in ***consumer goods***, the secured party must file this termination statement within a month of satisfaction of the debt, even if the debtor does not demand such a statement. (This special consumer-goods provision was added in 1972, on the theory that consumer debtors are often unaware of their right to clear the files, and of the importance of exercising that right. See §9-404, Reasons

for 1972 Change.)

E. Pre-filing: The secured party may sometimes want to file even before he has advanced money to the debtor. For if he waits until after the loan to file, there is a chance that some new security interest will be perfected before he has a chance to make his filing — under §9-312(5)(a) he would lose to this new interest.

 1. Rule allowing: Therefore, §9-402(1) allows the lender to file *before* he makes the loan, or even before the security agreement is signed. §9-312(5)(a) then gives him priority over any subsequently-filed interest, even if that interest was created, but not perfected, earlier (e.g., the other loan was made earlier). See the fuller discussion of pre-filing *infra*, p. 77.

F. Contents of financing statement: §9-402(1) sets forth several clear requirements for a valid financing statement. The large volume of litigation that has arisen concerning the contents of a financing statement virtually all arises from carelessness or ignorance on the part of the secured creditor.

 1. Formal requirements of financing statement: For most kinds of collateral, a financing statement is sufficient if it:

  a. contains the *names* of the debtor and secured party;

  b. is signed by the debtor;

  c. gives an address of the secured party from which information concerning the security interest may be obtained;

  d. gives a mailing address of the debtor;

  e. contains a statement indicating the types, or describing the items, of collateral.

  f. Special rules for real-estate-related collateral: Some special rules are imposed for certain collateral closely related to *real estate*. If the financing statement covers *timber* to be cut, *minerals* (including oil and gas), accounts from the sale of minerals at the wellhead or minehead, or *fixtures*, the financing statement must: (1) state that it is to be filed in the *real estate records* (which is the correct place for filing under all three alternatives of §9-401(1); see *supra*, p. 26); (2) contain a *description* of the real estate; and (3) give the name of the *record owner* of the real estate, if this is someone other than the debtor. All of these requirements (most of which were added in 1972) are designed to tie in with the real estate title-search methods commonly used. §9-402(5).

  g. Secured party's signature under 1962 Code: Under the *1962* Code (but not under the present Code), the *signature of* *the secured party* is also required on the financing statement. 1962 Code §9-402(1).

2. **Errors in financing statement:** In evaluating defects in the financing statement, §9-402(8) is of paramount importance: "a financing statement substantially complying with the requirements of [§9-402(1)] is effective even though it contains minor errors which are not seriously misleading."

   a. **Ambiguity:** This language gives rise to a major ambiguity: does it contain *two* conditions (that the errors be minor *and* that they not be seriously misleading) or merely one condition stated twice (implying that if an error is minor, it is not seriously misleading)? White and Summers (p. 954) state " . . . we think it likely that [the draftsmen] intended two conditions, and that subsection (8) does not save a financing statement which contains major but not misleading errors."

      Example: The debtor fails to sign a financing statement, but his name and address are clearly set forth on the statement, which is properly indexed. The omission is not seriously misleading (a third person is still put on notice that certain property of the debtor may be encumbered). Nonetheless, White & Summers argue that "the complete omission of one of the five conditions [for a valid financing statement] might still be called a major error." W&S, p. 945. And §9-402(8) would in that case not apply.

3. **What constitutes debtor's signature:** §9-9-402(1) provides that a financing statement, to be effective, must be signed by the debtor. While no court has squarely held that, under §9-402(8), the complete absence of a signature was "not seriously misleading", there has been much dispute about what exactly constitutes a signature.

   a. **Code definition of "signed":** §1-201(39) defines "signed" in a liberal manner: the term includes "any symbol executed or adopted by a party with present intention to authenticate a writing." Comment 39 to §1-201 makes clear the almost total lack of formalism in this definition: " . . . a complete signature is not necessary. Authentication may be printed, stamped or written; it may be by initials or by thumbprint. It may be on any part of the document and in appropriate cases may be found in a billhead or letterhead. No catalog of possible authentications can be complete and the court must use common sense and commercial experience in passing upon these matters. The question always is whether the symbol was executed or adopted by the party with present intention to authenticate the writing."

b. *Benedict* **case:** Some courts have followed the liberal policy implicit in the above Comment to §1-201(39) in determining what constitutes a party's signature on a financing statement. For instance, in *Benedict v. Lebowitz*, 346 F.2d 120 (2d Cir. 1965), the secured party typed his name and address in the appropriate place on a standard UCC financing statement form, but neglected to sign the statement due to a misunderstanding of the form's instructions. (The 1962 Code, requiring signature by the secured party as well as by the debtor, was in effect.) The secured party did obtain the signatures of the debtors.

    i. Holding: The court in *Benedict* held that the typewritten insertion by the secretary of the secured party at his direction of his name constituted a signing as required by §9-402(1). The court cited §1-201(39)'s definition of "signed", and held in effect that a symbol may be "executed" by typewriter.

4. Names of debtor and secured party: §9-402(1) requires the *names* of both the debtor and the secured party to be listed on the financing statement. A number of cases have arisen in which the name of one party (usually the debtor) appears incorrectly at least once on the financing statement — some cases have held the error to be minor and not barring perfection; others have held that the error does bar the financing statement from being effective. We shall consider three classes of "name error" cases.

    a. Statement properly indexed in spite of name error: If the financing statement contains a mistake in the debtor's name, but the filing officer has nonetheless somehow correctly indexed the statement (as where the debtor's name appears twice, once correctly), the courts have held that the financing statement is effective. W&S, 956-7.

        i. Rationale: In such a case, the chief function of the debtor's name requirement — indexing (§9-403(4) — has been accomplished.

        ii. *National Cash Register* **case:** For example, in *National Cash Register Co. v. Firestone & Co.*, 191 N.E. 2d 471 (Mass. 1963), plaintiff contended that the financing statement filed by the defendant was insufficient because it incorrectly described the debtor. The statement listed the debtor as "Carroll, Edmund d/b/a Cozy Kitchens . . . "followed by the correct business address. The plaintiff claimed that "Cozy" should have been "Kozy". The court held that this error was a "minor" one which was "not seriously misleading." (§9-402(8)). The court emphasized that since the debtor was an individual proprietorship, it was under his name, not the name under which he was doing business, that the financing statement should have been, and "for ought that appears, was" indexed. (§9-403(4) requires the filing officer to index the statement "according to the name of the debtor.") Therefore, the misspelling of the word "Kozy" would not have prevented a third person from finding the financing statement under Carroll's name in the public records. Once he found it, the word "Cozy" was close enough to "Kozy" to put that person on notice.

b. **Misindexed because of name error, but signature gave correct name:** If the debtor's correct name is given by his signature, but his name is misspelled or otherwise incorrect in the listing of his address and the filing officer incorrectly indexed the statement relying on the latter spelling, the courts split. White & Summers state (p. 957) that "partly because we are persuaded that few general creditors are misled by the misfilings which may occur as a result of the misspellings and misplaced names," the financing statement should be held valid where the debtor's signature discloses his correct name.

c. **Debtor's name not on financing statement at all:** There are some "name error" cases in which the debtor's correct name does not appear on the financing statement at all, and the statement is incorrectly indexed. This usually is because either the parties use the unregistered name under which the debtor does business, or because they are careless in not setting out the debtor's exact business name. This kind of error, when it leads to incorrect indexing, is not always "seriously misleading" — most courts have given decisive weight to *whether a reasonably diligent third party* searching the public record would have found the incorrectly filed statement. (For example, if the correct and incorrect versions differed only in the last letters of the name, so that the indexing was only slightly incorrect, the statement would probably be found and would thus not be "seriously misleading.")

> **Example 1:** A financing statement, filed by Bank, lists the debtor, Lintz West Side Lumber, Inc., as "Lintz, John Richard" and "Lintz, Mayella." Bank argues that since the debtor is a closely-held corporation in a small town, the filing under the names of the principal owners, directors and officers of the corporation was sufficient to provide notice to other creditors in the community.
>
> *Held*, the listing *was* seriously misleading, and Bank therefore loses. As a corporation, Lintz West Side Lumber, Inc. was a legal entity separate and distinct from John and

Mayella Lintz. A creditor would be justified in assuming that corporate assets would not be encumbered by a security interest filed against these individuals. Unless a creditor happened to request a search for security interests in the Lintz' personal property, Bank's lien would not be found. Therefore, the names listed were not sufficiently similar to the debtor's name to provide a creditor with reasonable notice of Bank's security interest, and the incorrect listing of the debtor was "substantially misleading." *In re Lintz West Side Lumber, Inc.*, 655 F.2d 786 (7th Cir. 1981).

Example 2: The financing statement lists the sole name under which the debtor does business, "Elite Boats, Division of Glasco, Inc.," rather than its legal corporate name, "Glasco, Inc." The former is the name: (1) under which the debtor has held itself out to the community and creditors; (2) used in its bills, contracts and telephone listing; and (3) found on its checks, stationery and bank account.

> *Held*, the listing *was not* seriously misleading. "[W]here the company does business only under one name, the opportunity for creditors to be misled is substantially reduced, even though that name is not the company's 'true name.' Under the circumstances of the case, any reasonably prudent creditor would have requested a search under 'Elite Boats' in addition to 'Glasco, Inc.'" *In re Glasco, Inc.*, 642 F.2d 793 (5th Cir. 1981).

Note: The dissent in *Glasco* argued that a creditor should be entitled to rely on a secured-party bank to list the debtor's legal name. As a result of *Glasco*, a case in which the trade name was not closely related to the legal name, it will now be necessary (the dissent contended) for creditors to anticipate mistakes by "would-be secured creditors" and conduct additional searches to avoid being judged as lacking in diligence.

d. Trade name not necessary: §9-402(7) (a new provision added in 1972), states that the financing statement need only list the individual, partnership or corporate name of the debtor, "whether or not it adds other trade names or the names of partners." Thus on the facts of *In re Glasco*, the secured party would have been much safer using the legal name (Glasco, Inc.) on the financing statement, and not mentioning the commonly-known trade name (Elite Boats).

e. Change in debtor's name: What if the debtor *changes his or its name*? A post-name-change creditor who doesn't know that the debtor used to have a different name will not know to look in the records under the old name, and will thus not be able to discover any pre-name-change filings. §9-402(7), added in 1972, gives the post-name-change creditor some, but not complete, protection; the second sentence of 9-402(7) provides that "where the debtor so changes his name or in the case of an organization its name, identity or corporate structure that a filed financing statement becomes seriously misleading, the filing is not effective to perfect a security interest in collateral *acquired by the debtor more than four months after the change*, unless a new appropriate financing statement is filed before the expiration of that time." In other words, the second creditor cannot be sure it is getting first lien on, say, a piece of equipment owned by the debtor, unless he makes sure that it was bought at least four months or more after any name change or change in corporate structure.

Example: In 1980, Edsel Motors gives First Bank a security interest in its after-acquired equipment. On Jan. 1, 1982, Edsel changes its name to Corvair Motor Co. On March 1, 1982, the company buys a large (and expensive) industrial robot. In 1986, Corvair gets financing from Second Bank, in return for a security interest in all equipment. Second Bank checks Corvair's title to the industrial robot (by checking the bill of sale, which is in the name of Corvair), and checks the public records, finding no security interest ever given by Corvair.

First Bank, not Second Bank, has priority in the robot, because the robot was bought less than four months after the name change. Thus even though First Bank did not lend in reliance on the existence of the robot, and Second Bank not only lent in reliance on that robot but did everything it could reasonably have done to check both title and public records, Second Bank loses out! See 53 Geo. Wash. L. Rev. 408 (quoted in S,S&W, pp. 123-24), arguing that this result is unfair. Also, observe that the same result would happen even if First Bank *knew* about the name change, and out of laziness (or even out of a desire to help Corvair defraud its new creditors) intentionally declined to file a financing statement with the debtor's new name on it. *Id.*

f. **Error in secured party's name:** The *secured party's* name, even though required on the financing statement, has nothing to do with indexing. Therefore, the test is whether "a reasonably prudent searcher can correctly determine the secured party from whatever information there is on the statement." W&S. P. 960.

5. **Errors in describing the collateral on financing statement:** §9-402(1) requires that a financing statement contain "a statement

indicating the types, or describing the items, of collateral . . . ”
While no case has concluded that a total absence of description was
nonetheless “not seriously misleading” under §9-402(8), a number of
cases have discussed what constitutes a sufficient description.

a. Cases where description is wrong: In some cases, the
secured party's adversary has claimed that the description on
the financing statement simply does not apply to the collateral
in question (usually because of the misuse of Code terms like
“general intangible” and “equipment”.) Except for the cases in
which the error is simply the incorrect listing of the serial
number of machinery, these cases have usually gone against
the secured party. W&S, 962.

Example: In *U.S. v. Antenna Systems, Inc.*, 251 F.Supp.
1013 (D.N.H. 1966), the court concluded that a payment of an
$8,000 sum to the debtor was a “general intangible”, and that
the security agreement and financing statement, which both
covered “contract rights” and “accounts”, did not describe this
collateral. This case will be discussed more fully *infra* at p.
52.

i. “Farm products”: Goods meeting the description of *“farm
products”* are not covered by a financing statement
describing collateral as “inventory” or “equipment.” §9-109.
“Farm products” include crops and livestock used or produced in farming operations, as well as products of crops or
livestock in their *unmanufactured* states, such as maple
syrup, milk and eggs. Controversy often arises over
whether the products of crops or livestock have been subjected to a “manufacturing” process and thus lost their
status as “farm products.” The Official Comment to §9-109
notes that an extensive canning operation is an example of
“manufacturing,” but that the pasteurizing of milk or the
boiling of sap to produce syrup is not.

Example: Debtor is in the business of producing eggs. The
eggs are collected, then cooled, washed, sprayed with oil to
seal the shells, candled, sized by weight, and packaged in car-
tons. Bank's financing statements and security agreements
cover Debtor's inventory and equipment, but not farm products.

Held, Debtor's eggs and chickens are “farm products”
pursuant to §9-109, not inventory. They are thus not subject
to Bank's security interest. Even though Debtor's methods
were sophisticated, and it produced only eggs, Debtor was
engaged in a farming, rather than manufacturing, operation.
Since the pasteurizing of milk and the boiling of sap to

produce syrup are not "manufacturing" (as the Official Comment to §9-101 notes), the washing, candling, and spraying of the eggs here was not manufacturing either. *In re K.L. Smith Enterprises, Ltd.*, 2 B.R. 280 (B.Ct.D.Colo. 1980).

ii. Other examples of misdescription: White & Summers list two other examples where misdescription of the collateral was held to render a financing statement invalid: " . . . 'premises' does not describe inventory or accounts receivable [*In re Weiner's Men's Apparel, Inc.*, 8 UCC Rep. Serv. 104] . . . and the description of a bankrupt's right to his tax refund (a general intangible under Article 9 according to the court) is not covered by a financing statement which claims only accounts receivabl. [*In re Certified Packaging, Inc.*, 8 UCC Rep. Serv. 95]." W&S, 962.

b. Where description is overbroad: Since the purpose of the "description of collateral" requirement is to enable the searcher to derive some meaningful information about what is (or at least, what is not) covered by a security agreement, the courts have sometimes held that a description was overly broad.

i. Courts liberal: However, broad descriptions are necessary for the operation of "after-acquired property" clauses. Therefore, it is only in exceptional cases, where it is apparent that the creditor was "in fact reaching for more than he had bargained for," (W&S, 964), that the courts have held financing statements invalid because of overly broad description. They are, however, likely to be somewhat stricter where only a "one-shot" deal, with no contemplation of after-acquired property, is involved. W&S, p. 963.

c. After-acquired clause not necessary in financing statement: Where the security agreement contains an "after-acquired property" clause, it is not necessary that the financing statement also mention such a clause.

Example: In the *National Cash Register* case, *supra*, p. 34, the financing statement referred to "all contents of [the debtor's] luncheonette . . . " and the secured party sought to enforce an interest against an after-acquired cash register. The court held that the description in the financing statement was adequate, since the register was equipment. The court noted that since the only purpose of the financing statement requirement was to put the searcher on notice that certain goods might be covered by a security interest, the listing of the "all contents of the luncheonette" was "enough to put the plaintiff on notice to ascertain what those contents were."

i. Undue specificity: But the financing statement, if it does not mention after-acquired property, must not be so specific that it negates the possibility that after-acquired property may be covered.

Example: Bank lends money to Printer. Printer grants Bank a security interest on his printing press; the security agreement lists the serial number of this press, and contains a clause granting Bank a security interest in "any other printing press that Printer shall hereafter acquire." Bank then files a financing statement, using the form suggested in §9-402(3). Under item 1 in the form, Bank places only the serial number of the press already owned by Printer. Printer subsequently buys another press, and gives a chattel mortgage on it to Creditor, who promptly files.

Creditor's security interest, not Bank's, will take priority with respect to the second press. §9-402(1) requires that a financing statement contain "a statement indicating the types, or describing the items, of collateral." The financing statement filed by Bank certainly does not indicate the types of collateral (it merely lists one particular printing press). Therefore, it is only valid if it described the "items" of collateral. Since it does not include the second press as one of the items, that press is not covered. Therefore, the interest in the second press is not perfected, and is subordinate to Creditor's security interest in that press, by §9-301(1)(a).

This example illustrates the dangers of unnecessary specificity in financing statements. If the financing statement filed by Bank had listed "Printing presses", an after-acquired press would have been covered, under the theory of *National Cash Register*. The term "printing presses" would be construed as a statement of the type of collateral, and would not not require updating when new presses were added. But if the statement purports to list items, rather than describe types, constant updating is necessary, unless an after-acquired property clause is present on the financing statement.

IV. SPECIAL PERFECTION RULES FOR PARTICULAR TYPES OF COLLATERAL

A. Scope of discussion: Not all means of perfection are allowable for all types of collateral. For instance, a security interest in an instrument cannot be perfected by filing (§9-304(1)). Conversely, a security interest in "accounts" cannot be perfected by possession. (§9-305; Comment 1 to §9-305). The following discussion describes the definitions of certain categories of collateral, and also treats the creation and perfection of security interests in these types. In particular, the discussion focuses on **"intangibles"** (that is, collateral other than "goods") — "documents", "instruments", "chattel paper", "accounts", "contract rights", and "general intangibles" are the major categories of intangibles.

B. Documents: Documents of title (referred to simply as "documents" in Article 9) are used where a carrier or storage-man of goods is involved. §1-201(15), which defines the term "documents of title", states that it includes **bills of lading, warehouse receipts**, dock receipts, "and also any other document which in the regular course of business or financing is treated as adequately evidencing that the person in possession of it is entitled to receive, hold, and dispose of the document and the goods it covers." Thus the holder of a bill of lading (initially, the person sending the goods) or of a warehouse receipt (initially, the person having the goods stored) shows the business world by his possession of the document that he can hold and dispose of the underlying goods.

1. **Conditions for document:** The last sentence of §1-201(15) states two conditions which a document must meet in order to be a document of title: (1) it must be issued by or addressed to a bailee (e.g. the trucker or warehouse company); (2) it must purport to cover goods in the bailee's possession which are either identified or are fungible portions of an identified mass (an example of the latter is "10 tons of corn", if the bailee has 50 tons of corn, any ton of which is fungible with any other ton.)

2. **Division into negotiable and non-negotiable:** Documents of title are divided into two categories: negotiable and non-negotiable. §7-104(1) provides that a warehouse receipt, bill of lading or other document of title is negotiable "if by its terms the goods are to be delivered to bearer or to the order of a named person." §7-104(2) states that any other document is non-negotiable.

   Example: A document which states "consigned to the order of A" is negotiable, as is one that reads "consigned to bearer." A document reading "consigned to A" is non-negotiable.

3. **Creation of security interest in document:** A security interest in either a negotiable or non-negotiable document, as in any intangible, is created by agreement, in the same way that an interest in goods is created.

4. **Perfection of security interest in documents:** With respect to perfection, the Code makes a sharp distinction between interests in negotiable, and in non-negotiable, documents.

   a. **Perfection of negotiable documents:** Where goods are subject to an outstanding **negotiable** document, "title to the goods is, so to say, locked up in the document and the proper way of dealing with such goods is through the document. Perfection therefore is to be made **with respect to the document**, and when made, automatically carries over to the goods." (Comment 2, §9-304, emphasis added.) Thus §9-304(2) provides that where the goods are in the possession of a bailee who has issued a negotiable document for them "a security interest in the goods is perfected by perfecting a security interest in the document . . . "

i. **Perfection by filing or possession:** §9-304(1) allows a security interest in a negotiable document to be perfected by **filing**, and §9-305 allows such an interest to be perfected by **possession**. Thus both goods and the document may be covered by the secured party's taking possession of the document, or by filing as to it.

Note: However, the clause from §9-304(2) cited above applies only as long as the goods are in the possession of the issuer of the document (the warehouseman, carrier, etc.) Once possession is given to someone else, the secured party must reperfect by perfecting his interest in the underlying goods themselves. This will be generally done by filing, unless the secured party gets possession of the goods.

ii. **Protection against buyers of goods:** If during the time that goods are held by a bailee and a negotiable document for them is outstanding, a security interest in the goods and one in the document are both perfected, the interest in the document takes priority (last clause of §9-304(2)). Since a security interest in a negotiable document may be perfected merely by the secured party's taking possession of the document, the result is that one who obtains a security interest in the goods from the bailor and obtains the negotiable document is assured that no interest perfected directly in the goods during the period the negotiable document was outstanding can be superior to his own interest.

iii. **Perfection by filing:** An interest in a negotiable document may be perfected by filing, as well as by possession as stated above. However, perfection by filing is much less desirable than perfection through possession — §9-309 indicates that a purchaser of a negotiable document will prevail over an earlier secured creditor who perfected his interest in the document by filing. C&K, 90.

iv. **Automatic temporary perfection:** Still a third method of perfecting an interest in a negotiable document is given in §9-304(4). This is the **"automatic perfection"** provision, which grants perfection for a **21 day period** to a secured party who has given new value under a written security agreement. §9-304(4) applies to instruments as well as negotiable documents, and is often used by banks to perfect a security interest in stocks against "day loans" made to stockbrokers. The "automatic perfection" rule requires neither filing nor possession during the 21 days.

v. Continued perfection where possession given up: Although §9-305 provides that a security interest that has been perfected by possession continues "only so long as possession is retained, unless otherwise specified in this Article", §9-304(5) lists several instances where a security interest continues for 21 days even though *possession* of the negotiable document is *surrendered to the debtor*. This "continued perfection" section is often used by banks who have issued letters of credit to importers, taken possession of a negotiable document covering the goods to be imported, and then wish to give the importer possession of the documents in order to allow him to sell the goods once they arrive. See W&S, 928. See also Comment 4 to §9-304.

vi. Illustration: The following Example illustrates the workings of the temporary and permanent perfection sections of Article 9, in a typical negotiable-document setting.

Example: On March 1, Bank lends Debtor $100, and takes a security interest in a bill of lading to the order of Debtor under a written security agreement. Bank does not take possession of the document. Bank wants to perfect its interest in the bill of lading.

The bill of lading is a negotiable document, since it is to the order of a named person (§7-104(1)(a)). §9-304(2) therefore applies; during the time the goods continue in the carrier's possession, "a security interest in the goods is perfected by perfecting a security interest in the documents, and any security interest in the goods otherwise perfected during such period is subject thereto." Thus Bank can protect itself, at least for the time the goods will remain with the carrier, by perfecting either by filing its interest in the document (§9-304(1)) or by taking possession of the document (§9-305). In any case, Bank gets a temporary 21-day period of perfection under §9-304(4), starting from the time its security interest attached.

Bank should, to protect itself permanently, do two things: (1) it should take possession of the document; if it does not do this, §9-309 creates the possibility that a third person to whom the document is duly negotiated will take clear title to the goods (see §7-502). (2) Bank should file as to the goods. If it does this, it will not have to worry that a security interest perfected in the goods after the carrier gives up possession will take priority as to the goods. (§9-304(2) gives priority to the perfected document interest over an interest perfected in the goods, only if the latter perfection occurs while the goods are in the carrier's possession, and this priority continues only while the carrier keeps possession.)

Now, suppose that on March 12, while the goods covered by the bill of lading are still in the carrier's possession, a creditor of Debtor levies on the goods; who has priority, Bank or the creditor? §7-602 provides that " . . . no lien attaches by virtue of any judicial process to goods in the possession of a bailee for which a negotiable document of title is outstanding unless the document be first surrendered to the bailee or its negotiation enjoined . . . " Thus as long as Debtor did not give the bill of lading back to the carrier before the goods were levied on, the creditor's lien on the goods is of no force. Again, Bank can guard against the possibility of Debtor's surrendering the bill of lading to the carrier prior to the creditor's levy, by taking possession of the document itself.

b. Perfection for non-negotiable documents: With respect to perfection of a security interest in goods covered by a ***non-negotiable*** document, the rule of "perfection of the goods through perfection of the document", used for negotiable documents, is ***not followed***. Instead, §9-304(3) allows the interest to be perfected through any of three methods: (1) filing as to the goods, (2) notifying the bailee (e.g. the warehouseman or carrier) that the secured party has a security interest, or (3) having a document in the name of the secured party issued to replace the document in the debtor's name.

    i. Filing preferable: Since the last two provisions listed above give a perfection that is only good for as long as the goods remain in the bailee's possession, most secured lenders will file as to the goods, since they will have to do this anyway once the goods leave the bailee's possession.

    ii. Continued perfection: §9-304(5), allowing continued perfection for 21 days if the secured party gives the debtor possession for certain purposes, applies to non-negotiable as well as negotiable documents. (§9-304(4), however, giving automatic perfection for 21 days where "new value" is given, does not apply to non-negotiable documents.)

5. Use of field warehouse receipts: At this point, a few words about one kind of non-negotiable document, the field warehouse receipt, are in order. Suppose a lender wishes to finance the inventory of a debtor, but wants to maintain substantial practical control over the debtor's disposition of the inventory. The secured party may elect to use a *field warehouse*; part of the debtor's premises would be transformed into a separate, locked area under control of an agent of the secured creditor. Notices would be posted stating that this area was a warehouse not under the debtor's control, and possibly a field warehouse company would be employed to run the warehouse. As the inventory purchased with the loan was delivered to the warehouse, the warehouse company would issue *warehouse receipts* (usually *non-negotiable* ones) in the secured party's name; the debtor would be allowed to sell the collateral only when the secured party surrendered the appropriate warehouse receipts. Thus the secured party has, in theory, complete control over what happens to the collateral, and can insist that the debtor surrender the proceeds from each sale.

   a. Bailor's rights when unauthorized sale made: §9-304(3) provides that if the bailee (the warehouse company) has issued non-negotiable documents for the goods (or no documents at all) the secured party can perfect its interest in the stored goods by filing as to the goods, or by notifying the bailee of the secured party's interest. See *supra*, p. 44. This arrangement, however, depends on the honesty and competence of the warehouse company. If the goods are unauthorizedly sold to third persons, it may be impossible for the secured party to recover them. §9-307(1) will give priority to any purchaser who is without knowledge that his purchase violates the security interest of the secured party. Also, even where the buyer is not protected by §9-307(1), practical considerations may prevent recovery. The goods may, for example, be untraceable and the debtor insolvent.

   b. *Procter & Gamble* case: This was in fact the situation in *Procter & Gamble Distributing Co. v. Lawrence American Field Warehousing Corp.*, 213 N.E. 2d 873 (N.Y. 1965), the famous "Salad Oil" case. The plaintiff, Procter & Gamble, sold vegetable oil to Allied, and held a purchase money security interest in it. The plaintiff shipped the oil to Allied's field warehouse, which was run by the defendant Lawrence American. The oil was to be held pending resale by Allied; non-negotiable warehouse receipts were issued by the defendant to the plaintiff. Allied went bankrupt without paying for the oil, and plaintiff then claimed the oil from Lawrence American, but most of it had disappeared. Since no one could determine where the oil had gone, there was no collateral for Procter & Gamble to repossess. The only thing it was able to do was to sue the warehouse company for conversion.

i. Suit against warehouse company successful: This conversion suit was successful. The court made two rulings of particular interest: (1) the warehouse company was forced to bear the burden of proving that it had never received the oil (a burden which it failed to meet); and (2) the measure of damages was "the highest value of the property between the date when the bailment commenced and the date when the bailor . . . received notice that the property had been lost."

C. Instruments.

1. **Perfection:** A security interest in an *instrument* (defined in §9-105(1)(i) to include negotiable instruments and securities) can be permanently perfected *only* by the secured party's taking *possession*. §9-304(1). For securities, see §8-321.

   a. **Exception for part of chattel paper:** The rule requiring perfection through possession does not apply to instruments which are part of *chattel paper*, that is, the promissory note which accompanies the security interest granted by the original debtor. (See p. 47.)

2. **Temporary perfection:** §9-304(4) allows perfection for a *21-day period* without possession or filing, if the security interest in the instrument arises for new value under a written security agreement. (See the discussion of automatic 21-day perfection for negotiable documents, *supra*, p. 42. Similarly, §9-304(5)'s "continued perfection" provision, *supra*, p. 43, applies to instruments.

3. **Negotiable instruments:** The Code distinguishes between negotiable instruments (given a fairly technical definition in §3-104) and non-negotiable instruments (which by §9-105(i) include "a security [i.e., a "stock"] (defined in §8-102) or any other writing which evidences a right to the payment of money and is not itself a security agreement or lease and is of a type which is in ordinary course of business transferred by delivery with any necessary endorsement or assignment.")

   a. **Perfection:** The rules for perfection are the same for both negotiable and non-negotiable instruments. However, the protection that the secured party obtains by perfecting is not the same for the two categories.

      i. **Protection for perfected interests in negotiable instruments:** §9-309 provides that "nothing in this Article limits the rights of a holder in due course of a negotiable instrument . . . or a bona fide purchaser of a security . . . and such holders or purchasers take priority over an earlier security interest even though perfected." If the secured party has possession of the negotiable instrument, he doesn't have to worry about a subsequent holder in due course — one must have possession to be such a "holder". If, however, the secured party gives the debtor possession of the instrument, relying on §9-304(4) or (5) for perfection, the debtor may *sell* the instrument, and the secured party may *lose to the holder in due course* under §9-309. Therefore, lenders should be wary of using §9-304(4) and (5) for negotiable instruments where they have any reason to mistrust the debtor.

ii. **Non-negotiable instruments:** Securities (defined in §8-102) are non-negotiable instruments by §9-105(i). §9-309 gives priority over a prior perfected security interest to bona fide purchasers of such securities. In this respect, the rights of secured parties in negotiable instruments and securities are the same. However, there are other kinds of non-negotiable instruments aside from securities — any of the writings evidencing a "right to the payment of money" (e.g. an ordinary I.O.U.) fall into this category. And certain purchasers of these other non-negotiable instruments are given superior rights by §9-308, which states that "A purchaser of . . . a non-negotiable instrument who gives new value and takes possession of it in the ordinary course of his business and without knowledge that the specific paper or instrument is subject to a security interest has priority over a security interest which is perfected under §9-304 [allowing automatic 21-day perfection (§9-304(4)) and continued 21-day perfection (§9-304(5))]." As in the case of negotiable instruments and securities, a secured party with possession does not have to worry — §9-308 gives superior rights only to bona fide purchasers who take possession.

D. Chattel Paper

1. **Definition:** Chattel paper is a writing that contains "both a monetary obligation and a security interest in or lease of specific goods." (§9-105(1)(b)). The term almost always refers to a *conditional sales contract* (which contains a promise to pay for goods and a security interest in the goods). The term is generally used only when the promise to pay and the security agreement in turn become the subject of a second security interest by the original secured party, who seeks new financing.

   Example: Dealer sells a tractor to Farmer on a conditional sales contract. Dealer then transfers the contract to his bank, either by outright sale or to secure a loan. (Article 9 applies to both sales of and security interests in chattel paper — §9-

102(a) and (b)). Since the conditional sales contract is a security agreement relating to specific goods, the contract is now the type of collateral called "chattel paper". In this transaction between Dealer and his bank, the bank is the "secured party", Dealer is the "debtor", and Farmer is the *"account debtor"* (defined in §9-105(a)).

Recall that by §1-201(37) a lease does not create a security interest unless intended as security. However, whether or not the lease itself here is a security agreement, it is chattel paper when it is transferred, if it relates to "specific goods". Thus, if Dealer enters into a straight lease of the tractor to Farmer (not intended as security), and then borrows money on the security of the lease, the lease is chattel paper. See Comment 4 to §9-105.

2. **Perfection of interest in chattel paper:** A security interest in chattel paper may be perfected either by *filing* (first sentence of §9-304(1)) or by the secured party's taking *possession* of the collateral (§9-305). Note that the account debtor's promise to pay is an instrument, and by §9-304(1) is the *only* kind of instrument that can be perfected by filing.

   a. **Rights superior to perfected security interest:** A perfected security interest in chattel paper is not superior to all conceivable interests in the underlying goods or obligation. Just as §9-307 gives priority over a perfected security interest in goods to a subsequent purchaser of the goods, §9-308 gives priority to a "purchaser of chattel paper . . . who gives new value and takes possession of it in the ordinary course of his business . . . if he acts without knowledge that the specific paper or instrument is subject to a security interest . . . "

      i. **Interest in chattel paper as proceeds from inventory:** §9-306 provides that where a perfected security interest in collateral covers "proceeds" of specified collateral, then a perfected interest arises in whatever is received by the debtor in return for the sale of the original collateral. However, §9-308(b) makes such a perfected security interest in chattel paper claimed as the proceeds of inventory inferior to the rights of a purchaser of the chattel paper who takes possession in the ordinary course of business and gives value, *even if* the purchaser knows about the security interest.

   Example: Auto Dealer gives Bank a security interest in all his inventory, and in "proceeds". Bank perfects by filing. Dealer then sells his cars on conditional sales contracts — the contracts are chattel paper, and they are covered by Bank's security interest, since they are proceeds from the sale of the inventory. Dealer then sells the chattel paper (or gives a security interest in it in return for a new loan) to Finance Co., which takes possession and which knows about Bank's security interest. §9-308(b) gives Finance Co. priority even if Finance Co.'s interest is only a security interest. Finance Co. is a "purchaser" by §1-201(32) in spite of the fact that it knew about Bank's interest.

b. Dangers of unperfection: The dangers of failing to perfect an interest in chattel paper (even an interest obtained by "buying" the paper) are shown in the following Example.

Example: Dealer sells a refrigerator to Buyer under a conditional sales contract that is duly filed; the refrigerator is for use in Buyer's factory. Dealer then sells the contract to Finance Co., which neither takes possession of the contract nor files a financing statement. A judgment creditor of Dealer levies on the refrigerator.

Finance Co.'s security interest is in chattel paper. Such an interest can be perfected either by filing (§9-304(1)) or by the secured party's taking possession of the chattel paper (§9-305). However, Finance Co. has done neither, and its interest is therefore unperfected. Therefore, Finance Co.'s interest in the chattel paper (and presumably in the refrigerator itself) is subordinate to that of Dealer's lien creditor under §9-301(1)(b). However, Dealer's lien creditor does not prevail over Buyer for the refrigerator, since Buyer has a right to possession of the refrigerator as long as he makes payments. Therefore, Dealer's creditor will probably levy on the chattel paper (thus taking prior to Finance Co. by §9-301(1)(b)), rather than on the refrigerator.

Now assume that a judgment creditor of *buyer* levies on the refrigerator; will he take prior to Finance Co? §9-302(2) provides that if a secured party assigns a perfected security interest, the interest continues perfected without filing against "creditors of and transferees from the original debtor." Since Dealer perfected its security interest in the refrigerator, perfection continues after the assignment to Finance Co., against Buyer's creditors.

Thus where Finance Co. does not perfect the assignment to it, it has priority over Buyer's creditors but not over Dealer's creditors. This result is set forth in Comment 7 to §9-302.

E. Accounts

1. **Definition of "account":** "Account" is defined by §9-106 to mean "any right to payment for goods sold or leased or for services rendered which is not evidenced by an instrument or chattel paper, whether or not it has been earned by performance."

    a. **"Contract rights" eliminated:** Under the 1962 Code, a distinction was made between "accounts" and something called *"contract rights"*. These were defined in 1962 Code §9-106 as "any right to payment under a contract *not yet earned by performance* and evidenced by an instrument or chattel paper." But under the 1972 Code, nearly everything that was a contract right under the old Code was placed within the category of an "account"; a right to payment for goods sold or leased or for services rendered (assuming that it is not manifested by an instrument or chattel paper) is therefore an "account", even if it has not yet been earned by performance.

    Example: Homeowner signs a contract with Builder, whereby Builder is to perform various major items of construction on Home-owner's house. The contract provides for progress payments, i.e., various amounts to be paid following the completion of certain amounts of work. Immediately following the signing of the contract, Builder's rights under that contract are an "account" under the present Code, even though he has not earned any right to payment yet. Under the old 1962 Code, his rights would be "contract rights" until, with respect to a certain sum, he earned the right to be paid by doing the work.

2. **Article 9 applies to sales of accounts and chattel paper:** Article 9 applies to "any sale of accounts or chattel paper." (§9-102(1)(b)). The only exception to this general rule is given by §9-104(f), which excludes from Article 9's coverage the "sale of accounts or chattel paper as part of a *sale of the business out of which they arose*, or an *assignment of accounts*, or chattel paper which is for the purpose of *collection only*, or a transfer of a right to payment under a contract to an assignee who is also to do the performance under the contract, or a transfer of a single account to an assignee in whole or partial satisfaction of a pre-existing indebtedness."

    a. **Rationale for application to sales:** Article 9 applies to many sales of accounts and chattel paper because of their *financing* aspects. For instance, consider the *factor*, who is really a lender, but who nonetheless sometimes buys accounts outright and without recourse (i.e., without the right to "charge back" against the purchase price the amount of uncollectable debts). Or, consider the *floor planner*, who finances a dealer's inventory, often in exchange for chattel paper which the floor planner buys without recourse. These factors and floor planners expect to take the account or chattel paper outright, and superior to the rights of the borrower/dealer's creditors. If they are to be allowed to do this, it is only fair that they be required to put their claims on the public record, so that other creditors of the borrower/dealer will know that these assets have been encumbered. See W&S, p. 894.

b. **Sales included in definition of "security interest":** Not only does Article 9 apply generally to sales of accounts and chattel paper, but the definition of "security interest" in §1-201(37) includes "any interest of a buyer of accounts or contract rights which is subject to Article 9." Thus the rules for filing, perfection and priority are the same for a buyer of an account as for a holder of a security interest in that account.

c. **Exceptions:** Keep in mind, however, the exceptions noted in Paragraph 2. For instance, in *Spurlin v. Sloan*, 368 S.W.2d 314 (Ky Ct. App. 1963), the owner of an account assigned it in order to pay off a prior debt. The assignee failed to perfect by filing. In a subsequent contest between the assignee and a creditor of the assignor who levied on the account, the court held in favor of the assignee. The court noted that "That assignment . . . was not a security transaction. . . . This assignment was an absolute assignment of a right to collect money due and owing. . . . We are of the opinion that no part of the . . . Uniform Commercial Code applies to a written assignment of funds presently due and owing for the purposes of liquidation or satisfying a prior existing obligation." (§9-104(f) was modified in 1972 to make it absolutely clear that assignment of an account in satisfaction of a prior debt is indeed excluded from Article 9's scope; Comment 6 to that section explicitly approves the result in *Spurlin*.)

3. **Perfection of interests in accounts:** §9-305 does not permit perfection by possession of accounts. Comment 1 to §9-305 explains that this is because this kind of property is "not ordinarily represented by any writing whose delivery operates to transfer the claim." (See the fuller discussion of the reasons for this bar *supra* at p. 24.) Therefore, a security interest in accounts may be perfected *only by filing* (§9-302).

a. **Exception for minor assignments:** The one exception to the above statement that interests in accounts may be perfected only by filing, is stated in §9-302(1)(e). That section exempts from the filing requirement (and allows automatic perfection of) "an assignment of accounts which does not alone or in conjunction with other assignments to the same assignee transfer a *significant part* of the outstanding accounts of the assignor. Thus the sale of an *occasional* account is perfected without filing or any other act of perfection beyond mere attachment of the security interest. However, where the assignor routinely assigns a significant portion of his accounts to a particular factor, this sale must be filed.

F. General Intangibles

1. **Definition:** *"General intangible"* is defined in §9-106 as "any personal property (including things in action) other than goods, accounts, chattel paper, documents and instruments." The term is thus a kind of "catch-all." The Comment to §9-106 states that the term applies to *"goodwill*, literary rights and rights to performance." Other examples given in that Comment, except to the extent that they are excluded from Article 9 by §9-104(a)'s exclusion for property regulated by federal statute, are "copyrights, trademarks and patents."

   a. **Sales not covered:** Although §9-102(1)(b) makes Article 9 applicable to sales of accounts and chattel paper, it does not extend Article 9 coverage to sales of general intangibles.

2. **Perfection of interest in general intangibles:** The only means of perfecting a security interest in general intangibles is by filing a financing statement. §9-302. (§9-305 does not permit perfection by possession — see Comment 1 to §9-305.)

3. *Antenna Systems* **case:** The distinction between "general intangibles" and "goods" was discussed in *U.S. v. Antenna Systems, Inc.*, 251 F. Supp. 1013 (D. N.H. 1966). The security interest in that case covered inventory, contract rights, accounts receivable, proceeds, and equipment. It did not, however, cover "general intangibles".

   a. **Blueprints are intangibles:** The court held that blueprints and drawings produced by the bankrupt debtor (an engineering firm) were general intangibles, not inventory or equipment. " . . . these blueprints, drawings, etc., [are] in reality the visual reproductions on paper of the engineering concepts, ideas and principles, [and] are general intangibles . . . not goods."

   b. **Bids and estimates are intangibles:** The court reached the same conclusion with respect to the bids, proposals and cost estimates rendered by the debtor.

   c. **Tooling was goods:** With respect to tooling (jigs, molds, templates, stampings), however, the court reached the opposite result: since the tooling was "used to manufacture" products sold by the debtor, this tooling was "equipment", not "general intangibles". The court cited Comment 5 to §9-109, which gives as examples of "equipment", "trucks, rolling stock, tools, machinery . . . "

V. CERTIFICATE OF TITLE ACTS

A. Exception for other filing systems: §9-302(3) exempts from the Article 9 filing requirements interests in property which are subject to certain non-UCC statutes. The exemption is primarily for the purpose of requiring that state *Motor Vehicle Certificate of Title acts* be followed. Non-UCC statutes providing for central filing of certain security interests are also deferred to, but few such statutes exist.

B. How Certificate of Title acts work: In nearly all states today, the ownership status of a *motor vehicle* is represented by a *Certificate of Title*. This Certificate is issued by the state as soon as the car is sold by the new-car dealer to a private party. Most of the Certificate of Title acts provide that *any security interest* in the automobile *must be noted on the Certificate of Title*. In these states, one may thus determine whether the vehicle is subject to a security interest merely by examining the Certificate of Title.

1. **Article 9 defers:** UCC §9-302(3)(b) defers to such a Certificate of Title scheme, where it exists. That section provides that the filing of a financing statement is neither necessary nor effective for perfection of a security interest if a Certificate of Title statute covers the vehicle in question. (However, an exception is made for a vehicle which is being held by a dealer as inventory, if the dealer as debtor creates a security interest in it.) But §9-302(3)(b) only applies where the state Certificate of Title *requires* that a security interest in the vehicle be noted on the Certificate. (The 1962 Code also contained an exemption where the Certificate of Title act *allowed* notation of a security interest on the Certificate, but did not require it. See 1962 Code §9-302(3)(b), Alternative B. This provision was dropped from the 1972 Code.)

   Example: State X has a non-UCC statute providing that a Certificate of Title must be issued for any car registered in the state, and that any security interest in the car must be noted on the Certificate by a public official. Consumer owns a car, in which he gives a security interest to Friendly Finance Co. Friendly must, in order to perfect, have an official (presumably from the motor vehicle department) note its interest on the Certificate. An Article 9 filing by Friendly would be both unnecessary and completely ineffective.

C. Conflict between dealer's creditor and buyer: A conflict may arise between a dealer's creditor, which has noted its interest on a Title Certificate, and a *subsequent purchaser* of that car. This conflict is discussed *infra,* p. 101.

VI. HOW THIRD PARTIES CAN GET DETAILS OF SECURITY AGREEMENT

A. Where third party desires further information: Suppose a third person examining the public records finds a financing statement indicating that there may be a security interest in certain goods of a particular debtor. Or suppose the third party learns that there may be a security interest from some other source. Since the third person cannot conclude from either the financing statement or other information that there definitely *is* such a security interest, he will often want to make further inquiries. §9-208 provides a procedure whereby he may seek information from the secured party through the mediation of the debtor.

   1. Secured party not required to divulge directly to third party: A financing statement is required to list an address for the secured party "from which information concerning the security interest may be obtained . . . " However, nothing in Article 9 compels a secured party to divulge any details to a searcher or other third party. Whether or not to divulge such information is left to the discretion of the secured party; as Comment 2 to §9-208 explains, " . . . the secured party should not be under a duty to disclose the details of business operations to any casual inquirer or competitor who asks for them."

   2. Debtor's right of inquiry: §9-208 does, however, give the *debtor* the right to obtain certain information and confirmation from his secured party. Thus if a third person contemplating a loan to the debtor makes it a condition of the loan that the debtor prove the nature and extent of any security interests he has already granted, the debtor can request the secured party to provide this information.

B. Mechanism of §9-208: By §9-208, the debtor may sign a statement "indicating what he believes to be the aggregate amount of unpaid indebtedness as of a specified date and may send it to the secured party with a request that the statement be approved or corrected and returned to the debtor." Thus the debtor can obtain from the secured party a statement showing exactly how much he owes the latter.

   1. List of collateral: Furthermore, "when the security agreement or any other record kept by the secured party identifies the *collateral*, a debtor may similarly request the secured party to approve or correct a list of the collateral." (§9-208(1)).

2. **Penalties for non-compliance by secured party:** §9-208(2) requires the secured party to comply with such a request by the debtor within two weeks, by sending a written correction or approval. If the secured party without excuse fails to do so, "he is liable for any loss caused to the debtor thereby."

   a. **Security interest limited:** Furthermore, if the debtor in his request for approval has included a good faith statement of the amount owed or of the collateral, and the secured party fails to respond, the secured party's security is limited to that shown in the statement as against persons "misled by his failure to comply." Thus if a third person lends to the debtor relying on the latter's statement that the secured party's interest only covers "inventory", and the secured party fails to respond to the debtor's good faith request to confirm this limitation, the secured party will be barred from enforcing a security interest in "equipment".

3. **Obligation to divulge successor in interest:** If the secured party no longer has an interest in the obligation or collateral at the time he receives a request for confirmation, "he must disclose the name and address of any successor in interest known to him and he is liable for any loss caused to the debtor as a result of failure to disclose." (§9-208(2)).

4. **Interest in all of a particular type of collateral:** "If the secured party claims a security interest in all of a particular type of collateral owned by the debtor he may indicate that fact in his reply and need not approve or correct an itemized list of such collateral." (§9-208(2)).

   Example: Secured Party has a security interest in all of Debtor's "equipment". Debtor, who is a baker, sends Secured Party a list of all his baking machines, and requests correction or approval. Rather than going over the list machine by machine, and ascertaining whether there are machines covered by the agreement not included in Debtor's list, Secured Party may simply note that his interest covers "all equipment."

5. **§9-208 not foolproof means of getting information:** §9-208(1) does not give a foolproof method of protecting third persons against false information about the security agreement. If the debtor submits a list of collateral for verification, the secured party is not required to respond if he does not have sufficient records identifying the collateral (unless the collateral is identified in the security agreement).

a. Debtor's obligation: Also, nothing in Article 9 requires the debtor to provide correct information, or any information at all, to a potential creditor or purchaser. (However, §1-203 imposes an "obligation of good faith" in the performance of all contractual obligations, and if a creditor lent money in reliance on false information provided by the debtor, he might have a cause of action for breach under this provision. Alternatively, an action might lie for misrepresentation.)

PERFECTION IN MULTI-STATE TRANSACTIONS

Introductory note: When a secured transaction has contacts with more than one state, where should the secured party perfect? Suppose, for instance, that the debtor is a corporation that is incorporated in Delaware, with its principal offices in New York, and that the collateral is in Chicago. Should the secured party file somewhere in Delaware, or somewhere in New York? Or Illinois? This chapter examines how the secured party chooses where to perfect in such cases of multi-state contacts. It also examines the situation in which a *second* filing is necessitated by inter-state transportation of the collateral, or by a change in the debtor's residence or place of business.

I. GENERAL PRINCIPLES

A. Five classes of collateral: The rules for perfecting in multi-state transactions are set forth in §9-103. That section is arranged on the theory that the rules for determining where to file against a particular sort of collateral should depend on the *nature* of that collateral. Therefore, separate rules are set forth for five different types of collateral: (1) documents, instruments and ordinary goods; (2) Certificates of Title; (3) accounts, general intangibles and mobile goods; (4) chattel paper; and (5) minerals. We follow this approach, and discuss the rules for each of these categories in turn.

1. **General rules:** Prior to this, however, it is possible to state two general rules that apply to all or most of the types of collateral. These general principles, stated in §9-103, Reasons for 1972 Change, are:

   a. **"Last event" rule:** The state whose law controls issues of perfection is the state where the *collateral is located* when the *last event* occurs on which is based the claim that the security interest is perfected or unperfected. Typically, this means that if a creditor is arguing that he has secured status, and he bases this argument on his having filed a financing statement, he will have to show that the collateral was located in the state where he did his filing at the time that filing took place (and that all other requisites of perfection had taken place before this).

      i. Exceptions: To this general "last event" rule, there are several exceptions, discussed in detail below. These include: (1) a provision involving purchase money security interests in goods, where the parties intend to remove the collateral to another state within thirty days after the debtor takes possession; (2) a provision that where the collateral is covered by a Certificate of Title, perfection will be controlled by the law of the issuing state; and (3) a provision that if the collateral is certain mobile goods or certain intangibles, perfection will be controlled by the law of the state where the debtor is located. See §9-103, Reasons for 1972 Change, Comment 2.

   b. Moved to another state: The second general rule is that where the collateral is *moved* from one state to another, the secured party has a *four-month grace period* within which to re-perfect in the new location. (In the case of accounts, general intangibles and mobile goods, the four-month grace period is triggered not by a transportation of the collateral, but by a change in the debtor's location.)

2. Conflict of laws: §9-103 is sometimes thought of as a "conflict of laws" provision. However, it performs only the limited function of telling the secured party *where to perfect* and *what happens if he doesn't perfect*. All other choice-of-law questions (e.g., which state's law controls on the issue of whether the description of the collateral in the security agreement is adequate) are controlled by §1-105(1), which in effect authorizes the state where suit is held to apply its own Code and Code-related case law to all transactions "bearing an appropriate relation to" that state.

   a. No right to vary: The rules of §9-103 (principally, as noted, rules governing where to file) *may not be varied* by agreement between the debtor and secured party. This is so, of course, because third parties (e.g., subsequent creditors) would not necessarily learn about the agreement, and would therefore not know where to check for filing or other perfection. By contrast, the secured party and creditor may agree that the law of any particular state having a reasonable relation to the transaction will govern as to other matters. Thus the parties might agree that the general Code statutory provisions and related case law of New York would apply to any controversy between them, if the secured party was a New York resident or company, and the debtor was a New Jersey company; but the parties could not agree that New York is the place where the secured party should file.

II. DOCUMENTS, INSTRUMENTS AND ORDINARY GOODS

A. **Items not ordinarily moved:** Certain types of collateral are normally kept in a *permanent location*. This is true of what the Code calls *documents*, *instruments* and *ordinary goods*. Essentially, all types of collateral except Certificates of Title, mobile goods, minerals, intangibles and chattel paper are covered within this broad classification. In the broadest sense, the rule governing perfection of an interest in these items is that one perfects *where the item is located* at the time one wishes to perfect.

B. **Language of §9-103(1):** The precise rule for perfecting such a usual item is given by §9-103(1)(b): "Perfection and the effect of perfection or non-perfection of a security interest in collateral are governed by the law of the jurisdiction *where the collateral is* when the *last event occurs* on which is based the assertion that the security interest is perfected or unperfected."

   1. **Summary of rule:** This means that at the time a creditor wishes to perfect, he must first ascertain where the items are located. He must then look to the law of that state to determine how and where to perfect. In the case of collateral which is to be perfected by filing, he will then file in the appropriate place in that state.

      Example: Debtor is a large corporation with its main office in New York City and a plant in Chicago. Debtor borrows money from Bank, and signs a security agreement giving Bank an interest in all of its equipment. This equipment includes its office furnishings in the New York office, and its machinery at the Chicago plant. Assuming that Bank wishes to perfect by filing (which is its only alternative except for taking possession of the collateral), Bank must file both in Illinois and in New York. That is, it will have a perfected security interest in the equipment contained in the Chicago plant only if it files in Illinois, and a perfected interest in the New York furnishings only if it files in New York.

   2. **Perfection by possession:** If the secured creditor wishes to perfect by *taking possession* of the collateral, the law of the state in which he is holding the collateral will apply as to the validity of the perfection, and the effect of non-perfection. Since all states except Louisiana have enacted Article 9, and since the provisions on perfection-by-possession have been kept uniform in nearly all states, serious issues under §9-103 are unlikely to arise where collateral of a sort that can be perfected by possession is indeed possessed by the secured party.

C. Movement of the collateral: In the case of ordinary non-mobile goods, as well as documents and instruments, we have seen that the rule is, in essence, "perfect according to the law of the state where the collateral is located at the time of perfection." But what if, after perfection, the collateral is *moved to another state*? If Bank takes a security interest in Printer's press when the press and Printer are in California, and Printer moves his whole operation to Illinois, is Bank's security interest to be considered valid in Illinois even if not filed there? Such an approach would not protect Printer's new Illinois creditors, who might well file a security interest in Illinois on the press, unaware that that interest would be subordinate to the California one. On the other hand, a rule that Bank's security interest became unperfected as soon as the press was moved to Illinois would be equally harsh to Bank, since Bank would need to make virtually continuous examinations to assure itself that the collateral was still present in California.

1. **Four-month grace period:** As a compromise between the competing interests of the original secured party, and the new actual or prospective creditors in the state to which the collateral is moved, the Code gives the original secured party a *four-month grace period* within which he must file in the new state. §9-103(1)(d) provides that the interest is perfected in the new state until: (1) four months after the collateral is brought into the new state; or (2) the expiration of perfection in the original state, *whichever happens first*. (Thus if perfection in the original state lapses before the end of the four-month period, perfection in the new state lapses as well.)

2. **Relation back:** If perfection in the new state occurs *within the four-month period*, the perfection *relates back* to the time of perfection in the original state.

   Example: Toymaker grants a security interest in his toy manufacturing equipment to Bank, which files in Massachusetts, where the equipment is then located. Later, Toymaker removes his entire operation, including the equipment, to Florida on January 1. On February 1, Toymaker takes out a loan from Finance Co., which files a security interest in Florida against the equipment. On March 1, Bank makes a new filing in Florida. Because Bank has filed in the new jurisdiction within four months of the transfer of the collateral, its security interest is deemed perfected as of the original date of the Massachusetts filing, and its interest has priority over Finance Co.'s security interest.

3. **When not filed in four months:** If the secured party does not perfect within the four-month grace period, his interest becomes *unperfected* at the end of that period. His interest is thus

subordinate to any security interest which is subsequently perfected, or to any judicial lien which subsequently arises. And if the debtor goes bankrupt after the four-month period, the security interest will be invalid against the bankruptcy trustee.

> **Example:** Seller sells two hydraulic cutting machines to Buyer on a conditional sales contract. The machines are in Seller's plant in New York at the time of the contract. The contract provides that the machines will be immediately taken by Buyer to its Pennsylvania plant, and that they will be kept there until fully paid for. Seller, relying on this provision, files only in Pennsylvania. Buyer, in plain disregard of the contract and without telling Seller, never takes the machines to Pennsylvania, instead installing them in its New Jersey plant. More than four months after Buyer has brought the machines into New Jersey, Buyer goes bankrupt, without Seller's ever having filed in New Jersey.
>
> *Held*, Seller's interest is invalid as against Buyer's bankruptcy trustee, because it was never perfected in New Jersey. Even if one assumes that the interest was validly perfected in Pennsylvania (which is not so, since the goods were not "mobile", and had to be perfected in the state where they were located at the time of perfection, not where the debtor's chief place of business was; see p. 65), Seller would have to refile in New Jersey within four months of the machines' arrival in that state. This is so despite the fact that Seller had no knowledge that the goods had been brought to New Jersey, and indeed had reason to think otherwise. *In re Dennis Mitchell Industries, Inc.*, 419 F.2d 349 (3d Cir. 1969).

a. **Filing after grace period:** Suppose that the four-month period expires, without the secured party's having re-perfected in the new state of location. If he perfects after that point, his perfection *does not relate back*, and instead dates only from the new time of perfection. If another secured party has perfected after the end of the grace period, and before the original secured party has perfected in the new state, the former will thus gain priority.

> **Example:** Bank takes a security interest in Printer's printing equipment, located at that time in New York. Bank files in New York. On June 1, Printer moves the equipment to Georgia. On October 15, Finance Co. takes a security interest in the same equipment, and files in Georgia. On November 1, Bank finds out that the collateral has been moved, and immediately files in Georgia. Under §9-103(1)(d)(i), Bank's security interest became unperfected in Georgia on October 1. Therefore, Bank's Georgia filing dates only from November 1,

and by the usual first-in-time priority rule of §9-312(5)(a), Finance Co.'s interest has priority.

b. New interest arises in four-month period: The above discussion assumed that the second interest arose only after the four-month period. But suppose that the second interest (perhaps a new secured creditor, or a lien creditor, or a trustee in bankruptcy) arises *during the four-month period*. At the particular moment where this new interest arises, the first secured party clearly has priority (assuming that his perfection in the original state has not lapsed for any reason). If the first party does not renew his perfection during the four-month period, who wins the priority conflict? It seems somewhat bizarre to say that the original secured party wins as long as the issue is litigated within the four-month period, but that the priority suddenly flip-flops at the end of that time.

   i. §9-103's language: §9-103(1)(d)(i) attempts to deal with this issue by stating that the first secured party's interest "becomes unperfected at the end of [the four-month] period and is thereafter deemed to have been unperfected as against a *person who became a purchaser after removal*."

   ii. Definition of purchaser: Since the words "purchase" and "purchaser" are defined in §1-201(32) and (33) to *include another secured party* and a *buyer who is not in ordinary course*, a priority dispute involving such claimants will indeed "flip-flop" — at the end of the four-month period.

   Example: Bank takes a security interest in Printer's equipment, located in New York; Bank duly files in New York. Printer moves the equipment to Florida on June 1. Offset Co., another printer, buys one of Printer's presses on July 1, in a transaction that is not in the ordinary course of the business of either Printer or Offset Co. As of July 1, Bank's security interest is still superior to Offset Co.'s rights in the press (since Offset Co., as a non-ordinary-course purchaser, does not get the benefit of §9-307's protection of a buyer in ordinary course; see *infra*, p. 96). But if Bank has not filed in Florida by October 1, or otherwise asserted its rights as against Offset Co. by that date, then Offset Co.'s rights suddenly become superior to Bank's on October 1. The same would be true if Offset Co. had lent money to Printer and filed a security interest in the press on July 1, instead of purchasing it.

   iii. Lien creditor or bankruptcy trustee: But the definition of "purchaser" does *not* include a *lien creditor*. And, since the rights of a trustee in bankruptcy are often premised upon his status as a lien creditor (see *infra*, p. 119), the trustee in a bankruptcy which ensued within the four-month period would also not be superior to that of the secured creditor. Thus if, in the above example, Printer went bankrupt on July 1, Bank's interest would be superior to the Trustee's, even if Bank never re-filed during the four-month period. See Coogan, §5B.06[3], p. 5B-61.

    iv. Mere assertion necessary: For the original secured party to prevail against an interest arising during the four-month period, it is probably not necessary that the secured party actually reperfect during the four months. All he must do is to **assert** his rights as against that new interest (e.g., by repossessing or attempting to repossess the collateral). As White and Summers state, "It makes sense to freeze the relative priorities inside the four-month period because that is when the conflict quickens. Thereafter, all that remains are settlement negotiations or trial. A refiling would add nothing." W&S, p. 974.

D. Goods to be kept in another state: It will often happen, particularly where purchase money security interests are involved, that the goods are in one jurisdiction at the time the security agreement is signed, but both parties contemplate that the goods will be moved to another state shortly thereafter. In such a situation, it is burdensome to the secured party to require him to file both in the state where the goods are then located, and in the state where they are to be moved. Therefore, §9-103(1) contains a special provision by which if the parties understand at the time the security agreement is signed that the collateral will be removed to another state, and it is in fact so moved within thirty days of the signing, the secured party **does not have to file in the original state**, and is protected both there and in the new state from the time he files in the new state.

    1. §9-103(1)(c): This provision is set forth in §9-103(1)(c): "If the parties to a transaction creating a **purchase money security interest** in goods in one jurisdiction understand at the time that the security interest attaches that the goods will be kept in another jurisdiction, then the law of the other jurisdiction governs the perfection and the effect of perfection or non-perfection of the security interest from the time it attaches until thirty days after the debtor receives possession of the goods and thereafter if the goods are taken to the other jurisdiction before the end of the thirty-day period."

        Example: Head Shops, Inc., located in New York, wants to order a large quantity of the latest craze in paraphernalia, the Pick Pot Pipe, sold by Pick Industries of California. Bank agrees to finance the acquisition, and lends Head Shops the purchase price. Without §9-103(1)(c), Bank would in effect have to file both in California and New York; if it filed only in New York, and did so before the goods arrived in New York, this filing would be the "last event" under §9-103(1)(b), which would make California the right place to file. If it filed only in California, and did so while the goods were still there, there would have to be a re-filing in New York within four months. If it waited until the goods arrived in New York before filing anywhere, it would run the risk of being beaten in a priority struggle by another secured creditor who filed in California or in New York, or by a lien creditor whose rights arose during the interim.

§9-103(1)(c) saves Bank from this dilemma. Since the transaction is a purchase money security interest in goods, and both parties intend that the goods will be transported from California to New York, Bank may simply file in New York. So long as the goods actually arrive in New York within thirty days of the New York filing, Bank's New York filing will be effective from the moment when it occurs. (But Bank must be careful that Head Shops indeed brings the goods to New York within thirty days. For instance, if Head Shops ships them to Illinois instead, and forty days after Bank's New York filing, Head Shops gives a security interest to a creditor who files in Illinois, Bank is out of luck.)

2. **Interest arising during thirty days:** As in the case of the four-month grace period, difficulties may exist where a new interest is created *within the thirty days*. The general rule for handling these problems is probably the same as in the four-month context; that is, the secured party must *assert his claim* as against the new claimant during the thirty day period, or lose.

> **Example:** Assume the facts of the above example. Suppose, further, that Head Shops ships the goods to Illinois, and that a creditor of Head Shops levies on the goods in Illinois less than thirty days after Bank made its New York filing. If, still within the thirty-day period, Bank begins judicial action to regain possession, tries to repossess itself, or perhaps even notifies the levying creditor of Bank's interest, Bank will probably win. This is because the conflict will be deemed "frozen" within the thirty-day period, and during that period Bank has a continuously perfected security interest dating from its New York filing. But if Bank does not assert its rights within the thirty days, the levying creditor's rights probably take priority on the thirtieth day. For a detailed explanation of why this is so, see W&S, p. 970.

III. MOBILE GOODS AND INTANGIBLES

A. Introduction: We turn now to the second of the classes of collateral listed on p. 57. This class is composed of *"mobile"* goods and of two types of *intangibles* (*"accounts"* and *"general intangibles"*).

1. **Mobile goods:** The term "mobile goods" is defined in §9-103(3)(a) to include goods which are "mobile and of a type normally used in more than one jurisdiction . . . if the goods are *equipment* or are *inventory* leased or held for lease by the debtor to others, and are *not covered by a Certificate of Title* . . . ." The section gives as examples motor vehicles, trailers, rolling stock, airplanes, shipping containers, etc. (assuming that the other requirements are met). This definition clearly *excludes* any vehicle used for *consumer* purposes, and excludes any vehicle for which a Certificate of Title has actually been issued.

   a. **Nation-wide usage:** In determining whether a given item of collateral is "normally used in more than one jurisdiction", the issue is whether users of that kind of equipment *in general* normally utilize the item in more than one state, not whether the particular debtor in question moves it from state to state.

      Example: The collateral consists of hydraulic cutting machines, which are normally used in a factory, and which in this case have been transported from the seller's plant in New York to the buyer's plant in New Jersey.

      Held, although the collateral is mobile in the sense that it can be moved, it is not "goods of a type which are normally used in more than one jurisdiction." The test for mobile goods "turns on the type of goods involved and not on their actual use in or transportation between more than one jurisdiction. *In re Dennis Mitchell Industries, Inc.*, 419 F.2d 349 (3d Cir. 1969) (other aspects of which are discussed *supra*, pp. 60-61).

B. Keyed to debtor's location: Mobile goods by their definition are likely to be shifted from one jurisdiction to another frequently. Intangibles have no physical existence at all. Therefore, as to both of these types of collateral, it is not sensible to make perfection depend on their location. Accordingly, §9-103(3)(b) chooses the state of the *debtor's location* as the place for perfection.

1. **Debtor's location defined:** §9-103(3)(d) contains a fairly precise definition of the debtor's "location": "A debtor shall be deemed located at his place of business if he has one, at his chief executive office if he has more than one place of business, otherwise at his residence."

   Example: Producer owns the copyright to Tops and Bottoms, a pseudo-pornographic revue. He induces Bank to finance the actual production, and Bank takes a security interest in the copyright. Producer has a small New York office, out of which work on this particular revue takes place. However, his main office is in California. The copyright is a "general intangible" (see *supra*, p. 52). Therefore, it falls within §9-103(3). Accordingly, Bank should file its security interest in the copyright in California, because this is where the debtor has his "chief executive office". §9-103(3)(d).

2. **Old Code has different rules for accounts:** Under the present Code, as noted, "accounts" are deemed intangibles, and are filed in the location of the debtor. But under the 1962 Code, a security interest in accounts (as well as in "contract rights", a term no longer used in the present Code) were to be perfected in the state "where the assignor of [the] accounts or contract rights *keeps his records concerning them....*" Because a creditor wishing to search the filings might find it difficult to determine the jurisdiction in which the assignor keeps his records concerning accounts or contract rights, this provision was dropped in the present Code; the searcher need now only know where the debtor is located.

3. **Change in debtor's location:** Suppose the debtor *changes his location* from one state to another. Just as a secured party whose collateral is, say, ordinary goods has four months in which to re-perfect in the new state, so the creditor whose collateral is a mobile good or intangible has *four months to re-perfect in the new state where the debtor has moved.* §9-103(3)(e) provides that "A security interest perfected under the law of the jurisdiction of the location of the debtor is perfected until the expiration of four months after a change of the debtor's location to another jurisdiction, or until perfection would have ceased by the law of the first jurisdiction, whichever period first expires."

   a. **Lapsed perfection:** As is the case with ordinary goods, the secured party who does not re-perfect under §9-103(3)(e) *loses his perfection* at the end of the four-month period. If he re-perfects subsequently, that perfection dates only from the moment of the new perfection.

IV. VEHICLES COVERED BY CERTIFICATES OF TITLE

A. **Problems of interstate movement:** As noted *supra*, p. 53, most states have Certificate of Title statutes, by which the only means of perfecting a security interest in a vehicle is to note that interest on the Certificate. Unfortunately, it is often possible for the unscrupulous to take a car covered by an encumbered Title Certificate in State One and obtain a new, clean Certificate in State Two; there are many states whose officials do not check for the existence of a Certificate on the car from other states. In view of the likelihood that cars will be transported from one state to another, there needs to be a system for determining whose state's Certificate applies. To a lesser extent, there is also a problem of handling a move from a Certificate state to a non-Certificate state, and vice versa. Certificate-to-Certificate moves are considered first, and limited attention to the other two situations is paid thereafter.

B. Certificate-to-Certificate: Assume that State One is a Certificate state, and that a Certificate is issued showing Secured Party's lien. Assume now that the car is brought into State Two, also a Certificate state.

1. **§9-103(2)(b):** This situation is dealt with by §9-103(2)(b), which provides: "Except as otherwise provided in this subsection, perfection and the effect of perfection or non-perfection of the security interest are governed by the law (including the conflict of law rules) of the *jurisdiction issuing the Certificate* until *four months* after the goods are removed from that jurisdiction and thereafter *until the goods are registered* in another jurisdiction, but in any event *not beyond surrender* of the Certificate. After the expiration of that period, the goods are not covered by the Certificate of Title within the meaning of this Section." (Emphasis added.)

2. **What this means:** This language apparently means that the State One Certificate is valid until one of the following things happens:

   a. the State One Certificate of Title is *surrendered* to a public official of State Two; or

   b. four months pass following the removal of the car from State One, or the vehicle is registered in State Two, *whichever comes later*.

3. **State One secured party protected:** To put it still another way, the original secured party whose interest was noted on the State One Certificate is protected by that Certificate for four months, so long as the Certificate is not surrendered to State Two officials. After the four-month period, the protection which the secured party obtains from his State One Certificate continues only until the vehicle is re-registered in State Two (even if the Certificate is never surrendered to State Two officials). Since surrender of the marked Certificate to State Two officials will almost always mean that the new Certificate issued by State Two will also show the original security interest (the only exception being a clerical error by State Two), the secured party normally has four months in which to inform State Two officials of his interest.

   a. **Consequence of failure to act:** If the secured party does not act within the four-month period, then the following bad things are likely to happen to him: (1) Once the four months have passed, and the car is re-registered in State Two, the State One Certificate will be of **no force**, and only State Two's Certificate will be effective. (2) Any buyer (whether a dealer or an amateur) who buys the car in State Two, whether during the four months or thereafter, will have priority over the original secured party. (3) A new creditor who takes a security interest which is noted on the State Two Certificate will take prior to the original State One secured party.

Example: Consumer buys a car in State A, and gets a loan from Bank. Bank has its security interest noted on a Certificate of Title issued by State A. Consumer moves the car to State B on January 1. On February 1, he gets a new State B Certificate of Title, by falsely telling State B officials that there is no outstanding Certificate from any other state. This State B Certificate, of course, does not reflect Bank's security interest. If Bank notifies State B officials by May 1 of its interest, then Bank will have priority over a professional buyer of the car (even one who actually relies on the clean State B Certificate of Title, and even if this reliance occurs before Bank has informed State B officials of its interest); also, Bank will take prior to any secured party who acquires an interest which it notes on the State B Certificate (again, even though the new secured party has relied on the clean Certificate). The only person who can defeat Bank is a non-professional (i.e., "amateur") buyer, whose status is discussed *infra*, p. 71.

If Consumer had surrendered its State A Certificate to State B officials on, say, February 1, the effectiveness of the State A Certificate would have immediately come to an end. Presumably, State B officials would have noted Bank's interest on the new State B Certificate, so that Bank would be continuously perfected. If, however, State B officials made an error, Bank would presumably be out of luck as against any buyer of the vehicle, or any secured party who noted an interest on the new Certificate.

Now assume that Consumer merely re-registered the car in State B, but neither surrendered the State A Certificate nor obtained a new State B Certificate. In that event, the State A Certificate remains the effective Certificate indefinitely (even after the four-month period). But once the four-month period has ended, the mere re-registering of the car in State B will terminate the effectiveness of the State A Certificate, and Bank's interest will become unperfected in State B. Then, any buyer will take free of Bank's interest.

To sum up, assuming that Consumer never surrenders the State A Certificate to State B officials, the State A Certificate loses its effectiveness upon registration in State B or the expiration of four months from the time the car left State A, *whichever occurs last*. Once that happens, any Certificate issued by State B would be the binding one, and if anyone buys against a clean Certificate, or notes a security interest on that Certificate, Bank will lose to that new interest.

4. **Theft:** Suppose the car against which there is a State One Certificate is *stolen*, and re-registered in State Two with a clean Certificate. The Code does not deal with this problem. However, the case law uniformly holds that the original secured party (whose interest is noted on the State One Certificate) has priority over post-theft buyers or secured parties. These decisions are reached as a matter of common law, based on the general theory that a thief cannot convey good title.

C. **Non-Certificate-to-Certificate movement:** Now suppose that the car is originally located in State One, which does *not* have a Certificate of Title statute, and that Secured Party perfects by filing. If the car's owner moves to State Two (a Certificate of Title state), and procures a clean State Two Certificate, what result?

1. **Four-month grace period:** Here, the applicable section is §9-103(2)(c), which keeps Secured Party's State One filing in force for *four months* following removal. That is, the situation is treated as if the collateral were ordinary non-mobile goods. If Secured Party manages to re-perfect in State Two within the four-month period, his perfection is continuous. If it is not, then he will lose to any purchase or security interest arising during the four months. Similarly, he will lose to any purchaser, or any interest noted on the Certificate, occurring at any subsequent time if Secured Party has still not perfected in State Two.

   a. **Secured Party's dilemma:** The practical problem for Secured Party in this situation is likely to be: how can I perfect in State Two? Since State Two is by hypothesis a Certificate-of-Title state, this perfection cannot be done by filing (as it was done in State One). The Certificate of Title statute of State Two is likely to provide that only notation on the State Two Certificate will suffice; Secured Party will probably have no practical way of getting hold of the State Two Certificate (except perhaps by threatening within the four-month period to repossess the car unless the owner tenders the Certificate). See Coogan, §30A.04[2], p. 30A-51.

D. **Certificate to non-Certificate movement:** Now consider the converse case: Secured Party perfects in state One by noting his interest on a State One Certificate of Title; the car is then moved by its owner to State Two, a non-Certificate state.

1. **Resolution:** The first step is to determine the period for which the State One Certificate continues to govern the transaction. This issue is resolved by §9-103(2)(b), exactly as in the Certificate-to-Certificate case. That is, the State One Certificate remains valid until either: (1) the State One Certificate is surrendered to State Two officials; or (2) four months pass or the vehicle is re-registered in State Two, whichever of these occurs last. If Secured Party can re-perfect in State Two (probably by filing) while his State One Certificate is still in force, he will be continuously perfected.

2. **Second step:** Assume now that it is determined that the State One Certificate has become ineffective under the above test. Now, §9-103(2)'s rules on Certificates of Title become irrelevant. Instead, the conflict is governed by §9-103(3), governing mobile goods, or by §9-103(1), governing ordinary goods (whichever is applicable to the type of vehicle in question).

> **Example:** Corporation buys a car in State A, and gives a security interest to Bank. Bank has this security interest noted on a State A Certificate of Title. On January 1, Corporation moves the car to State B, a non-Certificate state. If Bank files a security interest in State B by May 1, it will be continuously perfected from the date it noted its interest on the State A Certificate (assuming that Corporation does not surrender the Certificate to State B officials). After the four months, the State A Certificate will still remain in effect, until the car is registered in State B. Once registration in State B occurs (even though no new Certificate will be issued, since State B does not issue Certificates by hypothesis), the State A Certificate becomes immediately ineffective. Assume that re-registration occurs on June 1. As of June 1, the state in which perfection must occur is not the state where the car is located, but (since the car is a "mobile good" as defined in §9-103(3)(a)), the state where Corporation is located. If Corporation's chief executive office is in State *C*, perfection must occur in State C. Thus if State C is a Certificate of Title state, whoever is able to induce Corporation to obtain a new Certificate, and have his own security interest noted on it, will prevail; if State C is a filing state, whoever files first in that state will win.

E. Non-Certificate to non-Certificate movement: If neither state has a Certificate of Title statute (an unlikely event, since the vast majority of states have such statutes), §9-103(2) is entirely ignored. The collateral is treated either as ordinary non-mobile collateral (in which case one must re-file in the new state within four months, as discussed *supra*, p. 60), or as "mobile" goods, in which case one must make all filings in the state where the debtor is located (see *supra*, pp. 65-66).

F. The non-professional buyer: One of the purposes of Certificate of Title legislation is to enable a buyer to tell whether there are any liens against the car merely by inspecting the Certificate of Title. However, recall that often an unscrupulous owner may wipe out a State One Certificate showing liens by procuring a clean State Two Certificate. (Or, such an owner might purge a State One filing by procuring a clean State Two Certificate.) Since the secured party from State One has the opportunity to re-perfect in State Two within four months, this could leave the State Two buyer out in the cold, even though his State Two Certificate was clean. In the case of a State Two buyer who is a *professional* (one in the business of buying cars, i.e., a dealer), the Code draftsmen felt that the buyer should be able to protect himself. (For instance, he could quiz the owner about where the car came from, and he could check with officials of surrounding states.) But such a burden of inquiry would be crushing to a *non-professional* buyer (i.e., a consumer buying a used car). Therefore, §9-103(2)(d) gives such a buyer the protection he would expect to get from a clean Certificate.

    1. Requirements: The buyer who establishes his entitlement to §9-103(2)(d)'s protection takes free and clear of any security interest not noted on the State Two Certificate. For him to be entitled to that protection, he must satisfy the following requirements:

        a. the vehicle must be brought into State Two while a security interest in it is perfected (either by filing or by Certificate) in State One;

        b. a Certificate of Title must be issued by State Two after the car is brought there;

        c. this State Two Certificate must *not show* either: (1) that the vehicle is subject to the State One secured interest; or (2) that the vehicle "may be subject to security interests not shown on the Certificate";

        d. the buyer must *not be in the business of selling goods of that kind* (i.e., vehicles), he must give value, and he must take delivery of the vehicle after the State Two Certificate has been issued and without knowledge of the State One security interest. See W&S, pp. 985-86.

V. CHATTEL PAPER

A. Two ways to perfect: Recall that a security interest in *chattel paper* (e.g., the typical retail installment contract when used as collateral) may be perfected either *by possession* or *by filing*. (*Supra*, p. 48.) The multi-state provisions of §9-103(4), devoted solely to chattel paper, reflect this duality. If an interest in chattel paper is to be perfected by possession, the rules for documents, instruments and ordinary goods (*supra*, p. 59) apply; that is, perfection is governed by the law of the state where the collateral is possessed. If the interest is to be perfected by filing, the case is treated as if it involved accounts or general intangibles (*supra*, p. 65); that is, perfection must occur in the state where the debtor is located.

> **Example:** Car Dealer, whose office is located in California, sells much of his inventory on credit via retail installment contracts. To get financing, he gives an interest in the installment contracts (which are chattel paper vis-a-vis a secured creditor) to Bank. Bank wishes to file its security interest. It should file in California, because that is where Car Dealer is located. Then, Car Dealer borrows more money by giving an interest in the chattel paper to Finance Co., which takes possession of the paper at its home office in Oregon. Under §9-103(4), Finance Co. will be perfected in Oregon, since possessory interests in chattel paper must be perfected under the law of the state where the chattel paper is located (Oregon).
>
> Then, to determine whether Bank or Finance Co. has priority one leaves §9-103 entirely. The relevant section is §9-308, which gives priority to Finance Co. (even though it perfected after Bank) if Finance Co. can show that it: (1) gave new value; (2) took possession of the paper in the ordinary course of its business; and (3) acted without knowledge that the chattel paper was subject to Bank's interest. If Finance Co. fails to make these three showings, it will lose under §9-312(5)(a)'s general rule that the first to either file or perfect wins. (Bank could have protected itself by stamping the chattel paper with a notation "subject to a security interest held by Bank"; Finance Co. could then not have taken without knowledge of Bank's interest. See Comment 3 to §9-308.) See generally W&S, pp. 990-91.

VI. MINERALS

A. Location of minehead or wellhead: A security interest in *minerals* including oil and gas), which interest attaches before the minerals are removed from the ground or at the moment they are removed, is perfected according to special rules imposed by §9-103(5). That section provides that the law of the state *where the mine or well is located* governs; thus a creditor will normally file in the state where the mine or well sits. The same rule applies to a security interest in an *account* resulting from sale of the minerals at the wellhead or minehead.

1. **Transaction after extraction:** But the special rule for minerals applies only to interests arising *before or at the moment of extraction.* If Texaco sells gas to Dealer by making a delivery in a truck to Dealer, and takes a purchase money security interest, the special rule will not apply because the interest has not been created until after extraction and transshipment. Instead, §9-103(1) would apply to this gas (which would be "ordinary goods"), and perfection would be made by filing in the state where the gas is delivered to Dealer.

PRIORITIES

I. GENERAL SCOPE

A. Various kinds of conflicts: The secured party's major reason for taking a security interest is to be able to recover the money owed him if the debtor defaults. If the debtor has no other creditors, or only unsecured creditors, and has not sold the collateral to a buyer in ordinary course, this will be easy for the secured creditor to do. Part 5 of Article 9 gives the secured creditor both a right of "self-help" and also the right to foreclose on the collateral by use of judicial action. However, in many cases, there will be other interests held by third persons in the particular collateral upon which the secured party wishes to foreclose. In the case of a conflict between more than one property interest in given collateral, Article 9 usually establishes which of the competing interests has priority.

  1. Conflicts which may arise: There are a variety of interests which may compete with that of the secured creditor. He may, of course, be in conflict with the holder of another security interest in the same property. This other interest may either be perfected or unperfected. The secured party may also be competing with a person who has *purchased* the collateral, either in ordinary course or otherwise. Similarly, the secured creditor may be face to face with an unsecured creditor who has procured a *judicial lien* on the collateral, either by attachment, levy, judgment lien, etc. Or if the collateral in question is a *fixture*, there may be a third person who holds a real estate mortgage on the real property to which the fixture is affixed. In each of these situations, Article 9 resolves the dispute.

B. Importance of priority: Where two parties claim conflicting interests in given property, the usual result is that "the winning party satisfies himself *in full* out of the collateral before the subordinate party satisfies himself to *any* extent." W&S, 1031. Thus if the collateral when sold brings less than the amount of the winning party's claim, it is truly "winner take all".

C. Shelter principle: Article 9 sets forth a number of rules governing particular conflicts — these will be discussed below. In addition to these rules explicitly set out in Article 9, however, the reader should also be aware of the application of the common-law principle of *shelter*, which is applied to priority disputes.

  1. Definition: The common-law principle of "shelter" provides that the *buyer of property gets as good a title as his seller had*; the seller's title thus "shelters" the buyer's. This shelter principle is stated in §2-403(1) with respect to the sale of goods; however, it is not clear whether §2-403(1) can ever protect against a security interest. In any case, the common-law shelter principle applies against security interests by virtue of §1-103, which makes applicable the general principles of common law, unless they are specifically displaced by the provisions of the UCC. See W&S, 1031.

> **Example:** Secured Creditor takes a perfected security interest in Dealer's inventory, and the security agreement provides that buyers from Dealer do not take free of Secured Creditor's interest. Buyer 1 purchases the goods in the ordinary course of business; by §9-307(1) (discussed *infra*, p. 95), he takes free of the security interest, even though the security agreement provides otherwise. Buyer 1 then resells the goods to Buyer 2. The latter does not qualify under §9-307(1), because he did not buy from one in the business of selling goods of that kind, and is therefore not a buyer in ordinary course. Nor does he take free under §9-307(2) (*infra*, p. 99), because Secured Party has filed a financing statement covering the goods. Nonetheless, he takes free of Secured Party's security interest *because his seller took free*, and he gets as good title as his seller had. That is, he is "sheltered" by Buyer 1's title.

II. PRIORITIES BETWEEN CONFLICTING SECURITY INTERESTS

A. **Scope:** Not all security interests are created equal under the UCC. In addition to a marked discrimination against unperfected interests and in favor of perfected interests, the Code also gives special rights to certain *purchase money security interests*. The latter will be discussed *infra*, p. 79. For the moment, we will discuss only those conflicts between non-purchase money interests. We will, however, treat both perfected and unperfected interests.

B. **Residual rule of § 9-312(5):** Conflicts between two security interests are governed by §9-312, with the exception of certain cases governed by other sections and referred to in §9-312(1). §9-312 makes a basic distinction between cetain purchase money security interests and all other security interests. These purchase money interests are treated in §9-312(3) and (4). §9-312(5) is a kind of "residual clause", which governs all conflicts between secured parties not discussed in other parts of §9-312.

C. **Scope of §9-312(5):** The vast bulk of conflicts between secured parties are resolved by §9-312(5)(a): "Conflicting security interests rank according to priority in time of filing or perfection. Priority dates from the time a filing is first made covering the collateral or the time the security interest is first perfected, ***whichever is earlier***, provided that there is no period thereafter when there is neither filing nor perfection." (Emphasis added).

1. **Restatement:** Thus whichever secured party is the first to ***either*** file or perfect will have priority, so long as at all times thereafter there is either a valid filing or perfection. (This rule assumes that none of the competing interests is a purchase money security interest.)

   Example: Debtor is conducting loan negotiations with Bank and Finance Co. simultaneously. Bank has him sign a financing statement at the start of the negotiations, which Bank files on February 1. Finance Co. and debtor sign a security agreement on March 1, and Finance Co. lends money and files that same day. Bank lends in July, and Debtor signs a security agreement with Bank in August. Bank, not Finance Co., has priority. This is so because the first time there was either a filing or perfection was when Bank made its filing; thereafter, Bank at all times had either a filing or perfection.

   This is not really harsh to Finance Co. At the time Finance Co. made its loan, it could have checked the records, and could have seen that Bank was already on file. This system of priorities helps preserve the parties' ability to rely on the record.

2. **One interest not perfected by filing:** The same rule also applies where at least one of the interests has been perfected, but not by filing. The filer will take priority so long as the interest that was perfected other than by filing was perfected after the filer filed.

   Example: Collector begins loan negotiations with Finance Co. Finance Co. files a security interest in Collector's coin collection. Bank then makes a loan to Collector, signs a security agreement with him, and takes possession of the coin collection. Finally, Finance Co. makes a loan to Collector and obtains a signed security agreement. Finance Co. will have priority, even though Bank perfected (by taking possession) before Finance Co. perfected. This is because the first time there was either perfection or filing was when Finance Co. filed; since there was no subsequent time when Finance Co. had neither filing nor perfection, it continues to have priority. Bank could have examined the records before taking the pledge, and could thus have discovered Finance Co.'s prior interest.

3. **Knowledge irrelevant:** §9-312(5)(a)'s first-to-file-or-perfect rule applies ***regardless of the secured creditor's knowledge*** of the other security interest. That is, the first to file or perfect will win,

even though at the time he takes the final action necessary to consummate the security agreement, he knows about the other interest.

> **Example:** Consider the facts of the above example. Suppose that, at the time Finance Co. finally advanced money and obtained the security agreement, it knew that Bank had already taken possession of the collateral. ***Despite this knowledge***, Finance Co. will still have priority, because it was the first to have either a filing or perfection. To put it another way, §9-312(5)(a) is a *"pure race"*, not a "race notice", provision. See *Shallcross v. Community State Bank & Trust Co.*, 434 A.2d 671 (N.J. Super. Ct. 1981), to this effect. (But the court in *Shallcross* did acknowledge that the priority scheme set forth in §9-312(5) may be upset by a showing of ***bad faith*** on the part of the first-to-file creditor.)

4. **Rule protects ability to pre-file:** Perhaps the main rationale behind the "first to file or perfect" rule is that it facilitates the ***pre-filing of financing statements*** (that is, the filing of a financing statement before the security interest attaches — §9-402(1))

   a. **Explanation:** Under the first-to-file-or-perfect rule, a prospective party who has made a §9-402(1) pre-filing can rest assured that if no other financing statement was on record at the time he filed his own financing statement, ***no subsequently filed interest*** (except perhaps a purchase money one) ***can ever have priority***. He can then go ahead and make the loan under the pre-filed statement, without checking to make sure that no other secured party has perfected by filing in the interim.

   b. **Pre-filed interest still vulnerable:** But keep in mind that this protection given to the first to file is applicable only against a second interest that is a ***non-purchase money*** interest, and that is perfected by filing. A party who files at a time when no other financing statement is on record might still lose to an earlier interest which was already perfected, but perfected ***otherwise than by filing*** (e.g., by possession, or by temporary perfection under §9-304(4)).

   > **Example:** Collector pledges his coin collection to Bank on January 1, in return for a contemporaneous advance, and signs a security agreement at the same time. Bank's interest is thereby immediately perfected by possession. On February 1, Finance Co. checks the public records, finds no financing statement covering the collection, and files its own financing statement. At the same time, it makes a loan to Collector and obtains a signed security agreement. Even though the record

was clean when Finance Co. filed, it will lose to Bank; this is because the first perfection-or-filing was Bank's non-filing perfection.

Example: Debtor is the owner of a warehouse receipt (a negotiable document; see *supra*, p. 41). On February 1, Bank lends to Debtor against the security of this document, obtains a written security agreement, but does not take possession of the document. At this point, by §9-304(4), Bank's interest has become temporarily perfected, for a twenty-one day period. (See *supra*, p. 43.) On February 15, Finance Co. lends against the document, obtains a written security agreement, and files against the document. On February 18, Bank files against the document. Bank has priority; this is because the first act of perfection or filing was Bank's temporary perfection; Finance Co. loses even though at the time it filed it found a clean record (and even though it could verify that the document was still in Debtor's possession.)

However, if Bank did not file until more than twenty-one days after giving value (i.e., until after February 21), it would have lost its priority over Finance Co., because it would then no longer have been the case that Bank's interest was "continuously perfected" from the date it gave value; its claim would then date only from the date of its filing, which was subsequent to the date of Finance Co.'s filing. See generally §9-312, Comment 5, Example 3.

5. **Difference from old Code:** The present version of §9-312(5), which we have been discussing, is roughly similar to the 1962 version of that section. However, there is one difference worth noting. The 1962 version provided, in §9-312(5)(b), that interests would be ranked in the order of *perfection* unless both were perfected by filing. This meant that if one interest was perfected by filing and the other by possession, a different result might be reached than under the present Code.

Example: SP1 files a financing statement listing D as debtor before any security interest exists. This statement is filed on March 5, and covers all stock certificates owned by D. On April 1, SP2 executes a security agreement with D covering all of the stock certificates, advances money to D, and takes possession of the certificates. (SP2's interest in the certificates, which are "instruments", is perfected by the taking of possession — §9-305.) On May 1, SP1 executes a security interest with D covering the certificates, and lends money to D under the agreement. (SP1's interest is now perfected. This is so because it has both been filed against and has "attached"; attachment occurred when the agreement was signed, value was given, and the debtor had rights in the collateral; see §9-203(1).)

Under the old, 1962 version of §9-312(5)(b), SP2 would have priority, since it was the first to perfect. (The first to perfect wins, under the 1962 Code, when one or both of the interests is perfected otherwise than by filing.) Under the present, 1972, Code, §9-312(5)(a), SP1 has priority because it was the first party to *either* file or perfect; in this case, SP1 filed before SP2 either perfected or filed. Thus the result changes from the 1962 Code to the 1972 Code.

III. SPECIAL PRIORITY FOR PURCHASE MONEY SECURITY INTERESTS

A. **General priority principle:** The Code priority system reflects the feeling that one who by extending credit allows his debtor to obtain specific items deserves a special place in the priority system of Article 9 (a *"purchase money"* secured party under Code jargon), higher than that enjoyed by the ordinary secured creditor who merely makes a general loan against property already owned by the debtor. While the purchase money secured party does not get special rights vis-a-vis *all* third parties (for instance, he does not get special rights against third party ordinary course purchasers under §9-307(1)), he does get a preferred status against another Article 9 secured party if he complies with certain formalities set forth in §9 312(3) and (4).

1. **Rationale:** The principal rationale for granting exalted status to the purchase money lender or seller is that by so doing, a previously-encumbered debtor may be able to acquire new property and thus avoid economic strangulation.

   Example: Debtor, who is starting out in business, obtains a loan from Bank. Bank takes a security interest in all of Debtor's property, "now owned or hereafter acquired", in return for a $10,000 loan. Although Debtor has a satisfactory credit rating, Bank thereafter changes its policy and refuses to lend to any companies in Debtor's line of business. If no special provisions were made for purchase money security interests, Debtor might find that his ability to get additional credit was completely foreclosed, since no new lender or seller on credit would want to take subordinate to Bank's interest. With the special purchase money rules, however, Debtor can go to, say, Seller and say "Sell me new inventory on credit; your security interest will have priority, as to that inventory, over Bank." See W&S, p. 1043.

B. **Definition of purchase money security interest:** By §9-107, two classes of persons may become purchase money secured parties:

1. *sellers* who take a security interest to secure all or part of the purchase price of the collateral; and

2. other lenders who lend money for the purpose of allowing the debtor to obtain rights in the collateral, *if the money is in fact so used by the debtor.*

    a. **Cross-collateral agreement:** With respect to the first class of sellers, the purchase money security interest extends only to the extent that the collateral secures part of "its" (i.e., the collateral's) "price." (§9-107(a)) To the extent collateral secures a debt for the price of other collateral, that interest is *not* a purchase money security interest. See W&S, p. 1044.

        Example: Consumer buys ten different $100 items from Merchant on ten different conditional sales contracts. The contracts provide that no item shall be released from the security agreement until every item has been paid for. Merchant does not file a financing statement (relying on §9-302(1)(d)'s exemption from the filing requirements for "purchase money security interests in consumer goods.") Consumer then grants a security interest in all of his household goods to Bank, which perfects by filing. Consumer pays $500 of his $1,000 indebtedness to Merchant and defaults. What happens in a priority conflict between Merchant and Bank? To the extent that Merchant's interest is not a purchase money interest, it will lose to Bank, because its interest is unperfected.

        Some courts are likely to hold that Merchant's *entire* interest is not a valid purchase money security interest, because there is no way to tell which items are collateral securing which purchase price, and an interest is a purchase money interest only if it is secured by the item being purchased. This result was reached, for instance, in *In re Norrell*, 426 F. Supp. 435 (M.D. Ga. 1977).

        Alternatively, the court might conclude that only one-tenth of the value of each item secured its own price. This would yield only $100 worth of perfected purchase money security interests, and the rest would be unperfected; Merchant would thus take $100 of the collateral and bank would get the rest.

        The better way for Merchant to draft his installment contracts would be to specify that payments are to be first attributed to the earliest-purchased items. Merchant would then have a good chance of succeeding in showing that each item secured only its own purchase price, and that the whole debt was secured by purchase money interests. If Merchant had done this, he would now have a purchase money interest in the whole value of the five most recently purchased items, and would thus at least theoretically be fully secured. (Of course, Merchant could at least be assured of **perfected** status by **filing** as to each item, but this is probably prohibitively expensive. Furthermore, filing would do nothing to increase the likelihood that the interests will be held to be 100% purchase money security interests. To the extent that they are not purchase money security interests, they will lose to earlier-filed agreements containing after-acquired property clauses.) See W&S, p. 1044.

C. Nature of preference: Purchase money security interests receive special treatment under §9-312(3) and (4). Whereas as between two non-purchase interests, §9-312(5) gives priority to the first to either file or perfect, a purchase money security interest will often have priority even though it was both **filed and perfected after** a non-purchase money security interest in the same collateral was filed and perfected.

D. Inventory and non-inventory collateral distinguished: §9-312 distinguishes between purchase money security interests in inventory (which are treated in §9-312(3)), and purchase money security interests in all other kinds of collateral (treated in §9-312(4)).

    1. Definition of "inventory": §9-109(4) defines goods as "inventory" if "they are held by a person who holds them for sale or lease or to be furnished under contracts of service or if he has so furnished them or if they are raw materials, work in process or materials used or consumed in a business. Inventory of a person is not to be classified as his equipment."

        a. Broad definition: This definition of "inventory" is thus broader than the laymen's conception of the word, since it includes raw materials, work in process, and also items held for lease. "Thus, presumably, all of Hertz's rental cars are inventory, not equipment." W&S, 1049.

    2. Purchase money security interests in inventory: A purchase money security interest in **inventory** takes priority over any other security interest in that inventory, if the requirements discussed below are met by the purchase money secured party. There are two principal requirements which the purchase money party must meet: (1) one relating to perfection of his interest; (2) the other relating to **notification**.

        a. Perfection: The purchase money security interest must be **perfected at the time the debtor receives possession of the inventory**. In most cases, this will mean that the purchase money secured party has filed a financing statement before the debtor received the inventory. (However, if the goods are being held by a bailee, and the secured party authorizes them to be

released to the debtor temporarily for immediate resale or shipment, there may be temporary twenty-one-day perfection under
§9-304(5)(a)).

b. Notification: The purchase money secured party must also
give *written notification* to the holder of any *conflicting
security interest* in the same type of inventory, if the holder of
that conflicting interest *has filed a financing statement*.

   i. Time of notice: This notification must normally be made
by the purchase money party *before he files*. If the purchase money interest is to be temporarily perfected for
twenty-one days under §9-304(5), however, the notice must
be given before this twenty-one-day period starts, (i.e.,
before the goods are released to the debtor.) §9-312(3)(b).

   ii. Life of notice: The notice is *only valid for five years*.
That is, the notice must be given less than five years before
the debtor receives possession of the inventory to be covered
by the purchase money interest. §9-312(3)(c). This means
that the purchase money lender need give only one notice to
a conflicting secured party, and he may then make as many
purchase money loans as he wishes during the ensuing five
years.

   iii. Contents: The notice must state that the person giving it
has or expects to acquire a purchase money security
interest in inventory of the debtor, and must *describe such
inventory by item or type*. §9-312(3)(d).

   iv. Rationale for notice: The explanation for the notification
requirement lies in common financing practices. Typically,
the deal between an inventory secured party and his debtor
will require the secured party to make periodic advances
against new inventory receipts by the debtor. A dishonest
debtor might apply to the secured party for a new advance
even though he has already given a security interest in the
incoming inventory to a different secured party. The notice
requirement protects the inventory lender in this situation;
if he has received notice, he will probably not make the
advance, and if has not received notice, any advance he
may make will have priority. See §9-312, Comment 3.

c. Application to proceeds: The purchase money secured
party's priority clearly applies to the inventory itself. But does
that special priority position remain if the inventory is sold and
yields *proceeds*?

   i. Covers identifiable cash: Where the debtor sells the
inventory for *cash* which is received before or upon delivery

of the inventory, the purchase money interest priority *applies to these cash proceeds.*

Example: Debtor, in return for a general business loan from Bank, gives Bank a security interest in all of Debtor's inventory, equipment and cash, and the proceeds thereof. Bank immediately files. Finance Co. then lends Debtor money to purchase particular items of inventory, and takes a purchase money interest in this inventory; Finance Co. files before Debtor takes possession of the inventory. Debtor then sells some of the inventory items for $10,000 in cash. Finance Co. will keep its special purchase money priority over Bank as to the cash proceeds, because the cash was paid "before or upon" delivery of the inventory items to the buyer.

ii. **Accounts not covered:** But, and most importantly, the purchase money security interest does *not have special priority* as to proceeds which take the form of *accounts* generated upon sale of the item. Instead, a conflict between an interest in accounts claimed as the proceeds of a purchase money security interest in inventory, and an interest in accounts filed directly, is resolved by the general "first to file or perfect" rule of §9-312(5)(a). (§9-312(6) explicitly provides that the date upon which an interest in collateral is filed or perfected is also the date of filing or perfection as to the *proceeds* of that collateral.) Thus if one party files directly against the accounts, and the other perfects a purchase money security interest in inventory thereafter, any accounts generated by sale of the inventory will go first to the account filer, not the purchase money-inventory filer.

Example: Bank takes a security interest in Debtor's accounts, and files promptly. Then Debtor gives a purchase money security interest in certain inventory items to Manufacturer (who produces and sells the items); Manufacturer files a financing statement before Debtor receives the goods. (The security agreement automatically gives Manufacturer a security interest in the proceeds of that inventory, unless the parties have otherwise agreed; see §9-203(3)). Debtor then sells certain inventory items on credit to various third parties; these credit sales, of course, create "accounts". Bank, not Manufacturer, will have priority in these accounts. This is because: (1) the special purchase money priority does not exist as to the proceeds of the inventory sold, since this inventory was not paid for at or before the time the items were delivered to their buyers; (2) accordingly, the general "first to file or perfect" rule of §9-312(5) applies. Under that rule, since Bank was the first to either file or perfect (and actually did both before Manufacturer did either), it takes priority.

But, if Manufacturer had financed the particular inventory items **before** Bank had filed or perfected its security interest in the accounts, Manufacturer would have priority in the accounts. Again, this conflict would be resolved by §9-312(5), not the special purchase money priority. See §9-312, Comments, Examples 6-8.

E. Purchase money security interests in non-inventory: A purchase money security interest in **non-inventory** collateral can have priority over a conflicting prior interest even without notification to the other secured party. §9-312(4) gives priority to the purchase money security interest in non-inventory if it is **perfected at the time the debtor receives possession of the collateral or within 10 days** thereafter. (Note that this is the same "10 day grace period" that is given the purchase money lender with respect to lien creditors and transferees in bulk under §9-301(2)). Where the goods are "consumer goods," this purchase money security interest is perfected without filing under §9-302(1)(d).

1. **Reason for lack of notification requirement:** Comment 3 to §9-312 explains the reason for the lack of a notification requirement for non-inventory purchase money lenders: "Since an arrangement for periodic advances against incoming property is unusual outside the inventory field, no notification requirement is included in subsection (4)." (See the explanation of the purpose of the inventory notification requirement, *supra*, p. 82.)

2. **Priority over accounts:** Recall that where a purchase money security interest is in inventory, no special priority attaches to accounts that are created as the proceeds of the sale of that inventory. Where the collateral is **non-inventory**, however, proceeds from its disposition do have the same priority that the original collateral had. This difference is due to the fact that when a secured creditor finances directly against accounts, he is usually looking to accounts created by the sale of inventory, not accounts created from other sources.

   Example: Finance Co., in return for a non-purchase money loan, takes a security interest in Businessman's accounts. This interest is promptly perfected. Bank then makes a purchase money loan to Businessman to enable him to acquire a particular piece of machinery for use in the business (the machinery becoming "equipment"; see *supra*, p. 22). This interest is perfected. Businessman then sells the machine on credit (giving rise to an "account"). Since the machine was not inventory, Bank will keep the special purchase-money priority in the account even though it represents merely proceeds of the collateral to which the purchase-money interest attached. Thus even though Finance Co. filed first as to the account, Bank will prevail.

F. Where purchase money lender does not comply with §9-312(3) or (4): If the purchase money lender fails to comply with either §9-312(3) or (4) (e.g., he does not give notice in the inventory case, or he does not perfect within 10 days in the non-inventory case), his rights against a conflicting secured party are governed by §9-312(5). He is thus treated exactly the same as a non-purchase money security interest. If he is first to file or perfect, he wins. If not, he loses.

G. Where both secured parties qualify under §9-312(3) or (4): Difficulties arise if *both* secured parties qualify under §9-312(3) or (4). For instance, this may occur if a bank lends the down payment for a purchase, and the seller gives credit for the rest; each files within 10 days, and the goods are not inventory.

    1. Result unclear: It is not clear what happens in such a case. White & Summers state that "although one might argue that such creditors should share pro rata and neither receive priority, we believe that the proper rule is to go to the subsection (5) residuary clause and award priority to the winner there." W&S, 1052.

IV. RIGHTS OF UNPERFECTED SECURITY INTERESTS

A. Generally: We have seen that an unperfected security interest loses to a perfected interest, regardless of whether either or both is a purchase money security interest. However, there are some kinds of property interests against which an unperfected interest may be victorious. For example, an unperfected security interest will have priority over one who buys the collateral knowing about the security interest and knowing that his purchase violates that interest. See §§9-301(1)(c) and 9-307(1). This section will discuss the rules of priority governing conflicts between unperfected security interests and interests other than security interests.

B. General Rule of §9-201: The backdrop against which one must consider the rights of unperfected secured parties is given by §9-201: "Except as otherwise provided by this Act a security agreement is effective according to its terms between the parties, against purchasers of the collateral and against creditors." Thus in a conflict between a secured party, even an unperfected one, and some other interest, *the secured party wins unless the Act specifically provides otherwise*.

    Example: An unperfected security interest will have priority over the claim of a general (unsecured) creditor. See W&S, p. 1031.

C. Scope of §9-301(1): The basic listing of interests taking priority over an unperfected security interest occurs in §9-301. §9-301(1) makes an unperfected security interest subordinate to the rights of four classes of persons:

1. "Persons entitled to priority under section 9-312" (§9-301(1)(a))

2. "A person who becomes a lien creditor before the security interest is perfected" (§9-301(1)(b))

3. "In the case of goods, instruments, documents and chattel paper, a person who is not a secured party and who is a transferee in bulk or other buyer not in the ordinary course of business, or is a buyer of farm products in ordinary course of business, to the extent that he gives value and receives delivery of the collateral without knowledge of the security interest and before it is perfected" (§9-301(1)(c)) and

4. "In the case of accounts and general intangibles, a person who is not a secured party and who is a transferee to the extent that he gives value without knowledge of the security interest and before it is perfected." (§9-301(1)(d)).

D. Persons getting priority under §9-312: §9-301(1)(a)'s reference to "persons entitled to priority under section 9-312" covers all those classes of persons which by §9-312 have priority even over other perfected security interests. (E.g., certain purchase money security interests in inventory collateral, the first of two security interests to be perfected by filing, etc.) The classes of interests covered in those sections referred to in §9-312(1) also presumably get priority over unperfected interests by §9-301(1)(a). (E.g., ordinary course purchasers under §9-307(1)).

E. Levying creditors: §9-301(1)(b) makes the unperfected security interest subordinate to one who "becomes a lien creditor before the security interest is perfected." Thus, if the lien arises before the security interest becomes perfected, the secured party is not helped by perfecting subsequently (unless his interest is a purchase money security interest, in which case he has a 10 day grace period in which to file — §9-301(2). This is discussed *infra*, p. 87.)

1. **Definition of lien creditor:** §9-301(3) defines "lien creditor" to mean "a creditor who has acquired a lien on the property involved by attachment, levy or the like, and includes an assignee for benefit of creditors from the time of assignment, and a trustee in bankruptcy from the date of the filing of the petition or a receiver in equity from the time of appointment."

   a. **Explanation:** In other words, a creditor who has, even before gaining a judgment against the debtor, obtained an attachment of a given piece of property, gets priority over a security interest in that property if the lien creditor obtained the attachment before the security interest was perfected (if it ever was).

    i. Gap creditors not covered: Notice that the so-called "gap creditor," who extends credit between the time the security agreement is signed, and the time it is perfected, is not protected unless he also obtains a lien during this period. This represents a major change from the previous legislation of most states, which has protected the unsecured gap creditor even if he did not have a lien. This subject is treated more fully in the discussion of *Moore v. Bay, infra*, p. 130.

  b. Change from 1962 Code: Under the present Code, the lien creditor who obtains his lien before the security interest is perfected takes priority over that security interest, even if the lien creditor *knew* about the security interest when he obtained his lien. This represents a change from the 1962 Code, by which the lien creditor took priority only if he had no knowledge of the security interest at the time he obtained the lien. The change was made to reflect the general lack of importance of knowledge to Code priority conflicts (i.e., the "pure race" rather than "notice race" nature of the priority scheme. See §9-301, Reasons for 1972 Change.)

2. 10 day grace period for purchase money security interests: In spite of the fact that §9-301(1)(b) seems to give a lien creditor priority over any security interest if his lien arises before perfection, §9-301(2) makes an exception for *purchase money security interests*. That section states that "If the secured party files with respect to a purchase money security interest before or within 10 days after the debtor receives possession of the collateral, he takes priority over the rights of a transferee in bulk or of a lien creditor which arise between the time the security interest attaches and the time of filing."

  a. Transferees in bulk affected: The above section thus affects not only lien creditors whose lien arises between the debtor's possession and a filing made in the 10 day grace period, but also the rights of a *bulk transferee* (defined in §6-102) who buys during this same period. The rights of a bulk transferee and other non-ordinary course buyers will be treated in the discussion of §9-301(1)(c), *infra*, p. 130.

  Example: Manufacturer makes a conditional sales agreement with Businessman for a piece of industrial equipment to be used in the latter's business. Businessman receives possession of the equipment on August 1. On August 2, a judgment creditor of Businessman levies on the equipment. On August 10, Manufacturer files a financing statement covering the equipment. Manufacturer takes prior to the levying creditor under §9-301(2), since it filed within 10 days of Businessman's gaining possession, and its interest is a purchase money security interest. The same result would ensue if Businessman, instead of being levied upon, had on August 2 sold the major part of his equipment (including that sold to him by Manfacturer) and inventory to Buyer (who is thus a bulk transferee under §6-102(2)). Buyer would be inferior to Manufacturer under §9-301(2) just as the levying creditor is.

3. **Function of §9-301(1)(b) in bankruptcy:** §9-301(1)(b) is the most frequently used tool of the bankruptcy trustee seeking to invalidate an unperfected security interest. Section 544(a)(1) of the Bankruptcy Code gives to the trustee as of the date of bankruptcy the rights and powers of "a creditor that extends credit to the debtor at the time [of bankruptcy] and that obtains, at such time . . . a judicial lien on all property on which a creditor upon a simple contract could have obtained a judicial lien, whether or not such a creditor exists."

   a. **Practical effect:** Thus, the trustee gets all the rights that a hypothetical creditor with a lien on all the debtor's property would have under state law. If the state is a UCC state (as are all states but Louisiana), that hypothetical creditor would have priority over any unperfected security interest by §9-301(1)(b). The trustee can therefore couple §544(a)(1) with §9-301(1)(b) to take prior to, and effectively invalidate, any security interest not perfected as of the date of bankruptcy. This subject will be treated more fully in the discussion of bankruptcy, *infra*, p. 132.

4. **Workings of §9-301(1)(b):** The rights of levying creditors under §9-301(1)(b) are explained in more detail in the following Hypotheticals.

   Hypothetical 1: On Sept. 1, Factory makes a conditional sales contract with Retailer for 100 sets of golf clubs that are delivered to Retailer the same day. Factory duly files a financing statement on Sept. 15. A judgment creditor of Retailer levies on the clubs on Sept. 20. Who prevails, the creditor or Factory?

   §9-201 sets forth the general scheme of Article 9: "Except as otherwise provided by this Act a security agreement is effective according to its terms between the parties, against purchasers of the collateral and against creditors." Therefore, unless some other provision expressly subordinates

Factory's interest to the creditor's lien, Factory will have priority. No such provision makes Factory subordinate.

§9-301(1), which lists the interests to which an unperfected security interest is subordinate, makes that interest subordinate to "a person who becomes a lien creditor before the security interest is perfected." However, the lien creditor obtained his lien after, not before, perfection in this case.

Now, assume that the creditor levied on Sept. 12. In that situation, since the levying creditor levied before Factory perfected, §9-301(1)(b) gives him priority over Factory. (But note that 1962 Code §9-301(1)(b) required a lack of knowledge of the security interest by the levying creditor.)

Finally, assume that the creditor levied on Sept. 5, and Factory filed on Sept. 10. §9-301(2) provides that "if the secured party files with respect to a purchase money security interest before or within 10 days after the debtor receives possession of the collateral, he takes priority over the rights . . . of a lien creditor which arise between the time the security interest attaches and the time of filing." Factory's interest is a purchase money security interest; therefore, Factory has priority over the lien creditor, even though the latter's interest came into being before the perfection of Factory's interest. Thus the holder of a "purchase money" interest has a "10 day grace period" after attachment of his interest (usually when the debtor receives the goods — see §9-203(1)) in which to file. If he files within the grace period, he is protected against levying creditors (as well as against transferees in bulk, also covered by §9-301(2)) even if the latter obtain the lien prior to the secured party's filing.

Hypothetical 2: On Sept. 1, Volley, an amateur tennis player, bought from Manufacturer and took home with him a tennis racquet for his own personal use; the sale was made under a conditional sales contract. Manufacturer duly filed a financing statement on Sept. 15. On Sept. 20, a judgment creditor of Volley levied on the tennis racquet. Who prevails, the judgment creditor or Manufacturer?

The tennis racquet is consumer goods in Volley's hands (it is "used or bought for use primarily for personal . . . purposes" — §9-109(1)). Therefore, by §9-302(1)(d), no filing is necessary for perfection. Since Manufacturer's security interest attached when Volley took the tennis racquet home with him (§9-203(1)), it was perfected on Sept. 1 (see §9-303(1), which provides that a security interest is perfected "when it has attached and when all of the applicable steps required for perfection have been taken." There are no applicable steps for perfection here.

Note that although Manufacturer's security interest is perfected, and will be superior to any lien creditor's interest, it will not be superior to the rights of another consumer who ***buys*** the clubs from Volley without knowing of Manufacturer's security interest in them, unless Manufacturer ***files a financing statement*** prior to this second sale (§9-307(2)).

Hypothetical 3: Volley bought a tennis racquet for personal use. Later he borrowed money from Stringer, giving him a chattel mortgage on the racquet. Stringer did not file a financing statement for the tennis racquet. A judgment creditor of Volley then levied on the tennis racquet. Who takes priority, Stringer or Volley's judgment creditor?

Stringer's security interest is not perfected. §9-302(1) requires the filing of a financing statement for perfection of all security interests except those listed in that section; none of these exceptions is present here. (Stringer's interest is not a purchase money security interest in consumer goods, since it was taken neither by the seller of the collateral, nor by a person who gave value in order to enable the debtor to acquire rights in the collateral — §9-107.) Since Stringer's security interest was unperfected, it is subordinated to the rights of someone who becomes a lien creditor before the security interest is perfected. (§9-301(1)(b)) Therefore, as long as the judgment creditor did not know about Stringer's security interest, the creditor wins.

Hypothetical 4: Under a properly-filed conditional sales contract, Prince Racquet Corp. sold and delivered to Stringer a group of tennis racquets for use at Stringer's indoor tennis courts. Prince subsequently assigned this contract to Bank as part of a loan agreement. This assignment to Bank was not filed, and a judgment creditor of Stringer then levied on the tennis racquets. As between Bank and the judgment creditor, whose rights in the golf clubs prevail?

Prince originally held a perfected security interest in the clubs. §9-302(2) gives Bank the same protection against creditors of Stringer that Prince had — "If a secured party assigns a perfected security interest, no filing under this Article is required in order to continue the perfected status of the security interest against creditors of and transferees from the original debtor." Since Prince's perfected security interest has priority over a judgment creditor's lien, Bank assumes exactly the same rights that Prince had. Note, however, that §9-302(2) does not protect Bank against levying creditors of Prince. The assignment from Prince to Bank was an assignment of chattel paper (defined in §9-105(1)(b) as a "writing

. . . which evidences both a monetary obligation and a security interest in . . . specific goods.") Bank's own security interest in the chattel paper is not perfected against anyone except creditors and transferees of Stringer, and is subordinate to a levying creditor of Prince under §9-301(1)(b). Therefore, Bank should, to protect itself fully, file a financing statement listing its interest in the chattel paper (Comment 7, §9-302).

Now, suppose Bank had loaned Stringer the money to buy the racquets by crediting his account. If it took a written security interest in the racquets in return for the loan, but did not file, how would it fare against a subsequent judgment creditor of Stringer who had levied on the racquets? Bank's security interest is a "purchase money security interest" if it can show that the loan was in fact used by Stringer to buy the racquets. However, since the racquets are to be used by Stringer for business purposes, this is not a purchase money security interest in consumer goods, and must therefore be filed to be perfected. Since Bank's interest is unperfected, the levying creditor wins under §9-301(1)(b).

Hypothetical 5: Stringer bought a tennis racquet for his own use from Prince, under a conditional sales contract. Prince did not file a financing statement. Later, Stringer opened an indoor tennis club, and rented the racquet to his customers. A judgment creditor of Stringer levied on the racquet. As between Prince and the judgment creditor, who wins?

§9-109(1) states that goods are "consumer goods" "if they are used or bought for use primarily for personal, family or household purposes." Thus it is clear that at the time Stringer bought the racquet, and for as long as he used it for personal purposes, it was a consumer good. No filing was therefore necessary under §9-302(1)(d) as long as he used the racquet for personal purposes.

When he used the racquet in his business, however, it ceased to be a consumer good. The question thus arises, does a change in use which changes the status of the collateral affect any filing requirement? §9-401(3) states that "a filing which is made in the proper place in this state continues effective even though the debtor's residence or place of business or the location of the collateral or its use, whichever controlled the original filing, is thereafter changed." The Code draftsmen apparently overlooked the fact that no filing is required for purchase money security interests in consumer goods; §9-401(3) does not determine whether such an interest remains perfected when the use becomes non-consumer, since that section applies only to interests perfected by filing.

The rationale behind §9-401(3) is that " . . . the secured party would normally have no way of discovering such changes of use . . . " (1 Gilmore 598); therefore, it would be a great burden to saddle him with the consequences of non-perfection where such a change of use brought into play a different filing requirement (as might happen, for example, if a consumer good not subject to a purchase money interest became "equipment," and the jurisdiction had enacted the Second Alternative sub-section for §9-401(1)). This policy is equally applicable to the case here; it would certainly be unreasonable to expect Prince to follow Stringer around in order to make sure that he did not use the racquet for anything but personal purposes. Though note, however, that Prince had the option to "play it safe" by filing in all places it thought might conceivably be applicable.

On the whole, the Code's policy of not subjecting secured parties to unreasonable filing requirements, when coupled with the explicit policy of not requiring filing in the case of purchase money security interests in consumer goods, compels that Prince's interest be regarded as still perfected. Under the general principle of §9-201, Prince would then have priority over the judgment creditor. (If Prince's interest were found to be unperfected, it would be subordinate to that of the lien creditor by §9-301(1)(b)).

F. Transferees in bulk and other non-ordinary course buyers: §9-301(1)(c) gives priority over an unperfected security interest to a **transferee in bulk** (defined in §6-102 as a transferee of "a major part of the materials, supplies, merchandise or other inventory of an enterprise . . . ") to the extent that "he gives value and receives delivery of the collateral **without knowledge** of the security interest and before it is perfected." This section applies only to bulk transferees and other non-ordinary course buyers (*infra*, p. 93) who are **not** secured parties. Secured parties fall under §9-312.

1. **Two requirements:** The transferee in bulk must therefore, in order to gain priority over a security interest, (a) make some kind of payment (his priority extends only to the amount he actually pays), and (b) receive delivery of the collateral. He must do each of these things **without knowing** that the security interest exists and **before the interest is perfected**.

   Example: Jones buys the major portion of the assets of X corporation. The contract price is $10,000, and on March 1 Jones makes a down payment of $1000. He is unaware that X corporation had previously granted a security interest to Smith on February 15. Smith's security interest is perfected on March 2. Jones receives delivery of the assets of the business on March 3. If X corporation defaults on its obligation to Smith, Smith can enforce his security interest in the collateral, since §9-301(1)(c) does not protect Jones — Jones did not receive the collateral until after perfection of Smith's security interest.

Observe that this places a substantial burden on a bulk transferee in Jones' position; he is obligated to check the public records not only before making payment, but also before taking delivery; if he discovers that a security interest has been perfected after the time he made payment, he may be unable to get his money back, and will take subject to the security interest.

2. **§9-301(1)(c) applicable to other non-ordinary course buyers:** §9-301(1)(c) applies not only to transferees in bulk, but also to all other buyers not in the ordinary course of business. The term "buyer in ordinary course of business" is defined in §1-201(9) as "a person who in good faith and without knowledge that the sale to him is in violation of the ownership rights or security interest of a third party in the goods buys in ordinary course from a person in the business of selling goods of that kind but does not include a pawnbroker."

   a. **Non-ordinary course buyer:** An example of a non-ordinary course buyer who might be covered by §9-301(1)(c) is a person who buys a printing press from a printer. Since the printer is not "in the business of selling" presses, the purchaser is not an ordinary course purchaser and is thus not covered by §9-307(1), which allows a buyer in ordinary course to take prior to *any* security interest, perfected or not. See *infra*, p. 94. If the purchaser received the press without knowing that someone held a security interest in it, and before that interest was perfected, he would take free of the security interest under §9-301(1)(c) to the extent of value given.

3. **§9-301(1)(c) restricted to certain collateral:** §9-301(1)(c) applies only to goods, instruments, documents, and chattel paper. Comment 4 to §9-301 explains that the purpose of this limitation is to restrict the section to goods and to "intangibles of the type whose transfer is effected by physical delivery of the representative piece of paper." Accounts and general intangibles are covered not by §9-301(1)(c) but by §9-301(1)(d), which does not impose a requirement that the purchaser receive the collateral before the secured party perfects in order for the purchaser to have priority.

G. Buyers of accounts and general intangibles: A transferee of accounts and general intangibles takes prior to a security interest to the extent that he "gives value without knowledge of the security interest and before it is perfected." (§9-301(1)(d)). This section does not apply to transferees who are secured parties — they come under §9-312. This section is mainly used for non-ordinary course purchasers, since ordinary course purchasers of these items come under the full protection of §9-307(1), even as against perfected security interests.

H. **"Lack of knowledge" requirements:** §9-301(1)(b), (c) and (d) all protect a subsequent interest only if its holder takes his interest without knowledge of the security interest. This lack of knowledge requirement refers to *actual* knowledge, not constructive knowledge. Thus no matter how much reason the levying creditor, bulk transferee, etc., had to know about the unperfected security interest, he is not deprived of superiority unless he had actual knowledge.

V.　RIGHTS OF PURCHASERS OF COLLATERAL

A. **Generally:** We have seen above that certain purchasers of collateral not buying in the ordinary course of business take prior to the rights of an unperfected security interest. Certain other classes of purchasers of collateral obtain even greater rights under the Code. For example, a buyer in ordinary course takes prior to the rights of *any* secured party, perfected or not, under §9-307(1). Protection is also given to certain buyers of chattel paper and instruments (§9-308), buyers of negotiable instruments and documents (§9-309), and consumers who buy household goods from other consumers (§9-307(2)).

B. **Buyers whose purchase is authorized by the secured party:** There are, as stated above, a number of circumstances in which even a perfected security interest in collateral will be subordinate to the rights of one who has purchased that collateral from the debtor. One such situation is that in which the sale was *"authorized" by the secured party*.

　　1. **Consequences of authorization to sell:** §9-306(2) states that " . . . a security interest continues in collateral notwithstanding sale, exchange or other disposition thereof unless the disposition was authorized by the secured party in the security agreement or otherwise. . . ." In other words, if the secured party authorizes the debtor to sell the collateral, the secured party loses his security interest in the collateral, and the buyer takes free. (The secured party may, however, gain a security interest in the "proceeds" of the sale — see *infra*, p. 102.)

　　　　Example: General Motors makes a security agreement with Auto Dealer whereby GM sells inventory to Dealer on credit; each time Dealer makes a sale, a portion of the proceeds is to be paid to GM to reduce the outstanding debt. This arrangement, which is known as "floor planning," constitutes an *authorization* by GM to Dealer to sell the collateral. Therefore, any purchaser, no matter what his state of knowledge about GM's security interest, takes free of GM's security interest, by §9-306(2).

a. **Authorization through course of dealing:** Note that §9-306(2) speaks of authorization to sell the collateral being given "in the security agreement or *otherwise*." Thus even where the security agreement states that the collateral is not to be sold, if the *course of dealing* of the parties indicates that the secured party expects the collateral to be sold (as where the secured party tolerates such sales over a long period), "authorization" will be found, and the purchaser will take free.

Example: In violation of the terms of its security agreement with Secured Party, Debtor repeatedly sells secured cattle without Secured Party's consent or knowledge, and has payment checks issued in Debtor's name only. Debtor generally forwards such checks to Secured Party. Secured Party nevers objects to this practice. Debtor eventually encounters financial difficulties, and transmits the proceeds of some cattle sales to feed suppliers rather than to Secured Party. Following Debtor's filing for bankruptcy, Secured Party sues Debtor and Purchasers (who bought some of the cattle), claiming the unauthorized sales were in violation of its security interest and constituted conversion. Purchasers claim that Secured Party waived the sale restriction terms of the security agreement through its "course of performance."

Held, for Purchasers. Under §9-306(2), a security interest may be extinguished if disposition of collateral is authorized in the security agreement "or otherwise." Secured Party's lack of objection to the sales must be considered an " 'otherwise' authorization" of the sale, so Purchasers take the cattle free from the security interest. Also, any security agreement is an "agreement" as defined by §1-201, and any §1-201 agreement includes the bargain of the parties as found by implication from their "course of performance." Therefore, the parties' performance (Secured Party's acquiescence in the sales) resulted in the waiver of the express no-sale term in the security agreement. *National Livestock Credit Corp. v. Schultz*, 653 P.2d 1243 (Okla. 1982).

C. **Buyer in ordinary course:** If it cannot be determined that the sale of collateral was authorized by the secured party, §9-307(1) may nonetheless allow the purchaser to take free of the secured party's interest. That section gives priority to one who buys the collateral in the ordinary course of business; the priority exists *even over a perfected security interest*.

1. **Language of §9-307(1):** §9-307(1) states that "a buyer in ordinary course of business other than a person buying farm products from a person engaged in farming operations takes free of a security interest created by his seller even though the buyer knows of its existence."

2. **Conditions for §9-307(1)'s application:** White & Summers (p. 1067) list six conditions which a buyer must meet in order to take free of a prior perfected security interest by virtue of §9-307(1):

   a. He must be a buyer in *"ordinary course"* (the UCC does not define "ordinary course," but uses this term in §1-201(9)'s definition of "buyer in ordinary course of business");

   b. He must *not buy in bulk* and must *not* take his interest as security for, or in total or partial satisfaction of, a *pre-existing debt* (in other words, he must give *"new value"*);

   c. He must buy from one who is in the *business of selling goods of the kind bought* (that is, inventory, such as jewels from a jeweller, clothes from a haberdasher, etc.);

   d. He must buy in *good faith*, and *without knowledge* that his purchase violates anyone's ownership rights or security interest;

   e. The purchase must not be of farm products from a person engaged in farming;

   f. The security interest of which the purchaser is to take free must be one created by the seller himself (see *National Shawmut Bank v. Jones, infra,* p. 98).

      i. **Requirements contained in definition of ordinary course buyer:** Observe that criteria (a) through (d) above are all imposed by means of §1-201(9)'s definition of the term "buyer in ordinary course of business."

3. **State of buyer's knowledge:** §9-307(1) protects an ordinary course buyer "even though [he] knows of [the security agreement's] existence." Yet part of the definition of "buyer in the ordinary course of business" is that the purchaser must buy "without knowledge that the sale to him is in violation of the ownership rights or security interest of a third person. . . ." (§1-201(9) — see criterion (d) above). While these two provisions seem to be in conflict, they are really not. The buyer may know that a security interest in the goods exists, but he must not know that his purchase is in *violation* of that security interest. (That is, he must not know that the sale to him is "unauthorized" — *supra,* p. 94.) See Comment 2 to §9-307.

4. *Scott v. Apex*. The requirement that the purchaser not know that his interest violates a security interest was construed in *O.M. Scott Credit Corp. v. Apex, Inc.*, 198 A.2d 673 (R.I. 1964).

   a. Facts: The *Scott* case was a replevin action, in which the plaintiff Scott & Co. sought to recover garden products which one of its dealers, Mass. Hardware, had sold to defendant Apex.

   i. Sale to retailers prohibited: The security agreement between Scott and Mass. Hardware provided that the latter would only sell as a retailer, and not as a wholesaler. Apex, after discovering that this limitation would prevent Mass. Hardware from selling directly to it because it was a discount house, induced Mass. Hardware to sell to Old Colony without informing it that Old Colony was an Apex subsidiary.

   b. Basis of Scott's suit: When Scott discovered the unauthorized sale, it sued Apex to recover possession of the goods. Scott contended that it had a right of repossession because, under §9-306(2), (in the slightly different form in which it stood in the 1962 Code) "except where this Article otherwise provides, a security interest continues in collateral notwithstanding sale . . . by the debtor unless his action was authorized by the secured party in the security agreement or otherwise. . . ." Since the security agreement prohibited sale to retailers, Scott argued, its security interest continued in the goods after they were sold to Apex.

   c. Apex's "ordinary course buyer" defense rejected: Apex responded that it was protected by §9-307(1), since it was a buyer in ordinary course. The court found that Apex was not such an ordinary course buyer, because it failed to meet two of the requirements for that status: (i) It had not acted in good faith in soliciting the sale; and (ii) It knew that the sale was in violation of Scott's security interest.

   i. Distinction: The court acknowledged that §9-307(1) protects the buyer in ordinary course "even though [he] knows of the [security agreement's] existence". However, the court pointed out, here Apex not only knew that Scott had a security interest, but also knew that its purchase was in violation of that interest.

   ii. Court's conclusion: The court thus held that since §9-307(1) did not protect Apex, Scott's security interest continued in the goods after their sale under §9-306(2). Since Scott's security interest was valid, Scott was held to have rights in the goods superior to those of Apex, and it was therefore allowed to repossess.

    iii. Buyer without knowledge: Suppose that a customer of Apex bought the goods ***without*** knowledge of Scott's security interest; would it have prevailed against Scott? Assume that there was some event of default, such as non-payment by Mass. Hardware, which brought Scott's repossession right (§9-503) into play. In that event the buyer would ***not*** be protected. §9-307(1) allows a buyer to take free of a security interest only if it is "created by his seller." Since the security interest was created by Mass. Hardware, not Apex, §9-307(1) does not protect Apex's buyer. §9-306(2), which makes the security interest continue in collateral notwithstanding sale, would therefore give Scott a security interest in the goods bought by the buyer.

5. *National Shawmut Bank v. Jones*. §9-307(1) applies only to protect purchasers from security interests created by their sellers, and not to those interests created by others (for instance, by their seller's seller). This was the decisive factor in *National Shawmut Bank v. Jones*, 236 A.2d 484 (N.H. 1967).

    a. Facts of *Shawmut*: One Wever bought a car from Wentworth Motors under a conditional sales contract. A copy of the contract was filed, and the contract was assigned by Wentworth to the plaintiff Bank. Wever then sold the car to Hanson-Rock, a used-car dealer. The defendant, Jones, bought the car from Hanson-Rock in good faith and without knowledge of any security interest in the car. The plaintiff Bank sued Jones to recover possession of the car, claiming that its security interest continued in spite of the two subsequent sales which the car had undergone. The plaintiff also sought a ***money judgment*** for the amount owed on the car by Wever.

    b. Holding: The court held that §9-307(1) did not protect Jones, since that section only protects a buyer from a security interest "created by his seller." The Bank's security interest was created by Wever, not Hanson-Rock.

    i. §9-307(2) not applicable: Nor was §9-307(2), which covers sales of consumer goods, (and is discussed *infra*, p. 99), applicable to protect Jones. That section protects only those who purchase before the secured party has filed a financing statement. (It was apparently Wentworth, the original secured party, which filed the financing statement. By §9-302(2), this filing continued effective even after the assignment of the security interest to the plaintiff Bank.)

c. **Argument using §2-403 rejected:** The defendant purchaser also made an argument utilizing §2-403. §2-403(1) provides that " . . . a person with a voidable title has power to transfer a good title to a good faith purchaser for value. . . ." The defendant's argument was apparently that Wever had a voidable title, which then became a good title in the hands of Hanson-Rock and later in the defendant's hands. The court rejected this contention by noting that §9-306(2), which provides for the continuation of a security interest in collateral notwithstanding sale applies "except when this Article provides otherwise". Nothing in any Article other than Article 9 would therefore bar the security interest from continuing. The court also cited §2-403(4), which states that the rights of lien creditors are governed by Article 9, and §2-403(3), which states that Article 2 does not impair the rights of creditors of the seller under Article 9. White & Summers (p. 1074) find the court's rejection of the §2-403 argument "persuasive."

d. **Personal judgment against buyer granted:** The court in *Shawmut* held not only that the Bank's security interest continued in the collateral, but also that the defendant was *personally* liable on the portion of the original purchase price left unpaid by Wever. The court gave no explanation of this holding, and there does not appear to be any UCC provision which supports it. It seems extremely burdensome to subject a good faith purchaser to unlimited personal liability arising out of debts of his seller's seller. However, with respect both to the loss of the car and the personal judgment, the defendant has an action for breach of title warranty against Hanson-Rock under §2-312(1).

D. **Sales by consumers to consumers:** Suppose a consumer buys goods for his own personal use, and his seller takes a security interest in them (probably a purchase money security interest, automatically perfected under §9-302(1)(d). If the consumer then sells the goods to a second consumer, the latter is not protected by §9-307(1), since he has not purchased from one "in the business of selling goods of that kind." However, §9-307(2) may protect him.

1. **Terms of §9-307(2):** §9-307(2) provides that "in the case of consumer goods, a buyer takes free of a security interest even though perfected, if he buys without knowledge of the security interest, for value, and for his own personal, family or household purposes unless prior to the purchase the secured party has filed a financing statement covering such goods."

a. **Goods must be consumer goods in seller's hands:** Recall that whether goods are "consumer goods" or some other class of goods (e.g., "equipment") depends on the use to which the possessor puts them (*supra*, p. 22). The commentators have all concluded that for §9-307(2) to apply, the goods must be consumer goods ***both in the seller's hands and the buyer's hands***.

    i. Explanation: The requirement that the buyer must use the goods for consumer purposes is evident within the terms of §9-307(2) itself. The conclusion that the goods must be consumer goods in the seller's hands is less obvious. However, §9-307(2) starts by saying "in the case of consumer goods . . .", and then concludes with a requirement that the goods be consumer goods in the buyer's hands. Therefore, for the beginning of the section not to be superfluous, the phrase, "in the case of consumer goods" must mean "in the case of goods which are consumer goods in the seller's hands." See W&S, p. 1073, where it is stated that the section applies only to sales "by amateurs to amateurs."

b. Utility of section: §9-307(2) is used most frequently to protect secondary purchasers of collateral originally sold under purchase money security interests. The original purchase money interest is automatically perfected without filing, since it is in a consumer good; however, §9-307(2) enables the subsequent consumer purchaser to take free, if he does not know about the security interest when he buys. Of course, the secured party can protect himself against such a resale by filing a financial statement, but in most cases this is not worth the cost, since it is not usually feasible to go after the goods in the hands of a second buyer. Also, the likelihood of such a resale is in most cases fairly low.

E. Purchasers of chattel paper and non-negotiable instruments: A purchaser of chattel paper (*supra*, p. 47) or of an instrument (*ibid*) cannot take free of a security interest by §9-307(1), since that section requires him to be a "buyer in the ordinary course of business", and §1-201(9)'s definition of that term applies only to goods. However, §9-308 may protect him.

    1. Terms of §9-308(a): By §9-308(a), a purchaser of chattel paper or of an instrument takes free of a filed or temporarily perfected security interest in the paper or instrument if he has done three things:

        a. given *"new value"* (the term is not defined in the Code, but one who takes the paper or instrument to secure a pre-existing debt, although he has given "value" under §1-201(44)(b), has not given "new value." §9-108 gives several examples of new value.);

b. taken possession of the paper or instrument in the ordinary course of his business (note that he doesn't have to be a "buyer in ordinary course of business," but must merely buy in the course of his *own* business); and

c. taken without knowing that the paper or instrument is subject to a security interest.

2. **Proceeds of inventory:** If a purchaser of chattel paper or of an instrument fails to be protected by §9-308(a) because he knew of the security interest, he still takes free of an interest "which is claimed merely as **proceeds of inventory** subject to a security interest." (An interest in proceeds arises under §9-306(2) — *infra*, p. 102.)

> **Example:** Appliance Dealer buys its inventory of washing machines from manufacturer on credit. A security interest between the two gives Manufacturer a security interest in the washing machines, and also recites that "proceeds" are covered. The security interest is duly perfected by filing.
>
> Dealer than sells several of the machines on credit to consumers, who execute conditional sales contracts. Dealer sells these contracts at a discount to Factors Corp. (The contracts constitute chattel paper in Factors Corp.'s. hands). Factors Corp. knows that the contracts are proceeds of the sale of Dealer's inventory, and that they are thus covered by Manufacturer's security interest.
>
> Under §9-308(b), Factor Corp. takes the contracts free of Manufacturer's interest, since the latter was claimed "merely as the proceeds of inventory." It wins despite its knowledge of Manufacturer's security interest. (The result would be the same if Factors simply took a security interest in the contracts rather than buying them, if it took possession — §1-201(32) makes a secured party a "purchaser".)

3. **Old Code:** The 1962 Code did not give §9-308 protection to negotiable instruments. Also, only chattel paper, not non-negotiable instruments, got the benefit of what is now §9-308(b).

F. **Purchasers of negotiable documents, negotiable instruments, and securities:** By §9-309, a secured party is subordinate to the rights of the holder in due course of a negotiable instrument (given under §3-302), to those of a holder of a negotiable document to whom the document was duly negotiated (§7-501), and to those of a bona fide purchaser of a security (§8-301). These purchasers have priority even though the security interest is perfected.

G. **Purchasers of vehicles:** Special problems may arise when there is a contest between an *automobile dealer's* secured creditor, and a *purchaser of the car* from the dealer's inventory. If the jurisdiction has a

Certificate of Title Act in force, and the dealer's creditor has perfected by noting its interest on a Certificate of Title (e.g., a special dealer's Certificate of Title), the secured party will typically argue that the existence of a Certificate of Title Act removes the transaction entirely from Article 9. Therefore, he argues, the perfection requirements of the Certificate statute are the only ones applicable, and perfection accomplished in this manner is good even against a subsequent purchaser. The subsequent purchaser, on the other hand, will argue that §9-302(3)(b) only exempts secured parties from the *filing* provisions of Article 9, not from the other aspects of that Article. Thus, the purchaser argues, §9-307(1) gives an ordinary-course purchaser priority even over a security interest which became perfected by notation on the Certificate.

1. ***Sterling Acceptance* case:** The purchaser prevailed in such a contest in *Sterling Acceptance Co. v. Grimes*, 168 A.2d 600 (Pa. 1961). The Court agreed that §9-302(3)(b) indeed only exempted the secured party from Article 9's filing requirements, not from its rules on subsequent **bona fide** purchasers.

2. **Used car vs. new car:** The car in *Sterling* was a new car. The court in *Sterling* hinted that had a used car been involved, the equities might have been different; the purchaser of a used car generally expects to have the Certificate of Title produced before he buys, and it is less unfair to bind him to the contents of that Certificate of Title even if he never sees it. However, White and Summers state that even in this used car situation, "the trend favors the purchaser" from the dealer, rather than the dealer's secured creditor. W&S, pp. 1076-77.

   Note: But if the used car is sold *by a private party* to another private party, the holder of a security interest noted on the Certificate of Title will almost certainly prevail over the buyer. Under §9-307(2), the buyer in an "amateur-to-amateur" sale loses if the secured party has previously "filed a financing statement covering the goods". A court would almost certainly construe the notation of a security interest on the Certificate of Title as constituting the equivalent of such a filing, so that even by the explicit terms of §9-307(2) the buyer would lose.

VI. PROCEEDS

A. **Generally:** Suppose that Bank has a perfected security interest in Auto Dealer's inventory of cars. If one of these cars is purchased by a buyer in ordinary course, that buyer has priority over Bank's security interest by §9-307(1). Thus, Bank has effectively lost a valuable item of collateral. The purchaser may have paid for this car in a variety of ways: he may have executed a conditional sales contract ("chattel paper" under

§9-105(1)(b)); he may have paid cash; or he may have traded in his old car. §9-306 grants Bank a way of gaining a perfected security interest in the cash, the chattel paper, and the used car. All of these items are known as "*proceeds*."

B. "Proceeds" defined: §9-306(1) defines "proceeds" to include "whatever is received upon the sale, exchange, collection or other disposition of collateral or proceeds. . . ."

    1. "Cash proceeds" vs. "non-cash proceeds": §9-306(1) establishes two classes of proceeds. *Money, checks* and *bank accounts* are "*cash proceeds*". All other types of proceeds are "non-cash proceeds." The distinction becomes important in the event of insolvency, treated by §9-306(4) (discussed in the treatment of bankruptcy, *infra*, p. 149).

C. Proceeds automatically covered by agreement: It is not necessary for the security agreement to state explicitly that proceeds are covered. By §9-203(3), "Unless otherwise agreed a security agreement gives the secured party the rights to proceeds provided by Section 9-306." However, as this provision indicates, the parties are free to specify in the security agreement that proceeds will not be covered.

    1. Change from old Code: This automatic proceeds provision represents what is probably a change from the old, 1962 Code. The 1962 Code did not explicitly state whether a proceeds interest is automatically created where the security interest remains silent, but a negative answer was implied (by 1962 Code §9-203(1)(b), which stated that "In describing collateral, the word 'proceeds' is sufficient without further description to cover proceeds of any character.")

D. Insurance payments as proceeds: *Insurance payments* received as a result of loss or destruction of the collateral generally constitute "proceeds". §9-306(1) provides that "Insurance payable by reason of loss or damage to the collateral is proceeds, except to the extent that it is payable to a person other than a party to the security agreement." Thus in the usual case, where the insurance policy lists the beneficiary as being either the debtor or the secured party, the secured party will have a security interest in any payments made by the insurer. But if some other person were listed as the payee under the policy (e.g., another creditor), the terms of the policy would be carried out, and the secured party would not gain any interest in the payment.

    1. Change from 1962 Code: The explicit classification of insurance payments as proceeds represents a change from the 1962 Code. The 1962 Code was silent on this issue, and a number of courts considering the question held that insurance payments from loss or destruction of collateral were not proceeds. See, e.g., *Universal CIT*

Credit Corp. v. Prudential Investment Corp., 222 A.2d 571 (R.I. 1966).

E. Perfection of interest in proceeds: A secured party is given an interest in proceeds by §9-306(2), as noted. But the question whether this interest in proceeds is **perfected** is governed by §9-306(3).

1. **3 Methods:** Under §9-306(3) there are three distinct ways in which an interest in the proceeds may become perfected:

   a. **Same type of collateral:** First, suppose that a financing statement has been filed covering the original collateral, and that the proceeds are of a type such that that financing statement, filed in the place where it was actually filed, is the appropriate means of filing. In this situation, the original financing statement **covers the proceeds as well;** no additional filing is necessary. (Nor is it necessary that the financing statement explicitly mention that proceeds are to be covered.)

      Example: Bank finances Dealer's inventory of new cars, and files a financing statement in Dealer's inventory. This financing statement is filed in the appropriate place (probably the secretary of state's office.) Then, Dealer sells one of the new cars to Buyer, and takes Buyer's used car as a trade-in. Since a used automobile held by Dealer is inventory, and a security interest in that used car could have been perfected by filing a financing statement in the secretary of state's office, the original financing statement covers the used car as well as the new cars. Thus no further filing or other action by Bank is necessary to perfect its proceeds interest in the used car.

      If, however, Dealer had sold the new car in return for Buyer's promissory note (a negotiable instrument), the original financing statement would no longer constitute adequate perfection. The reason for this is that filing is never an appropriate means of perfecting an interest in a negotiable instrument (see §9-304(1)), and the filing thus would not have been adequate to perfect an original interest in the negotiable instrument. Accordingly, Bank would have a ten-day grace period (see *infra*, Paragraph c), and after that would have to perfect by taking possession of the promissory note.

   b. **Identifiable cash proceeds:** Secondly, the secured party's proceeds interest will be perfected if a filed financing statement covered the original collateral, and the proceeds are "identifiable **cash** proceeds" (i.e., money, checks, deposit accounts, and the like). But this interest is perfected only as long as the debtor holds onto the cash. If he uses that cash to buy something else, the previous paragraph must apply; furthermore, in the case of "proceeds . . . acquired with cash proceeds", there is an additional requirement that "The description of collateral in the financing statement *indicates the type of property constituting the proceeds* . . . ." §9-306(3)(a).

Example: Suppose the same facts as the above example, but Dealer sells one of the new cars for cash. He then takes this cash and spends it on office equipment. This office equipment will be covered as proceeds from the disposition of Bank's collateral only if the original financing statement filed by Bank states something like "This financing statement covers all proceeds of disposition of covered collateral, whether such proceeds be equipment, inventory or consumer goods." (This requirement of description in the financing statement is to protect other creditors; otherwise, another creditor of Dealer would think that Dealer's office equipment was unencumbered, since there would be no reason to suspect that that equipment was covered under a financing statement listing only "inventory" as original collateral.)

   i. Certificates of deposit are not "cash proceeds": At least one court has held that *certificates of deposit* are *not* "identifiable cash proceeds" within the meaning of §9-306(1) and (3)(b). *Citicorp (USA) v. Davidson Lumber Co.,* 718 F.2d 1030 (11th Cir. 1983). CD's are not money or checks, and are specifically excluded from the definition of "deposit account" in §9-105(1)(e). In light of this exclusion, it defies logic to suggest that CD's are to be treated as cash proceeds, the *Citicorp* court held.

c. Ten-day grace period: Thirdly, for *ten days* after the debtor disposes of the original collateral, the proceeds are perfected (assuming that the interest in the original collateral was perfected.) This is true no matter what the nature of the proceeds is and no matter what the nature of the perfection of the original collateral was. Thus in the next-to-previous example, Bank's interest in the promissory note remained perfected for ten days after Dealer's receipt of it, even though the original financing statement was inappropriate to perfect an interest in a negotiable instrument.

   i. Re-perfection: But following the ten-day grace period, the secured party must perfect an interest in the proceeds *as if they were original collateral*, assuming that neither of the two means of perfection (a valid financing statement or coverage of identifiable cash proceeds) applies. Thus in the promissory-note-as-collateral example, within ten days of the time Dealer took possession of the promissory note,

Bank must take possession of that note (since possession is the only means of perfecting an interest in a negotiable instrument.) If it does so within this time, its interest is deemed continuously perfected. If it waits until after the ten-day period, its interest will only be deemed perfected from the time it takes possession (so that it might lose to an intervening interest, such as a levying creditor.)

2. **Change from 1962 Code:** The present version of §9-306(3), discussed above, differs in one particularly important respect from the 1962 Code. Under the 1962 Code, a filed financing statement covering original collateral was sufficient to cover proceeds only if the financing statement *explicitly mentioned* proceeds. This was usually done by means of checking a box marked "proceeds" on the financing statement; since virtually every secured party automatically checked the "proceeds" box, the draftsmen of the '72 Amendments decided simply to dispense with the requirement that proceeds be explicitly mentioned. See§9-306, Reasons for 1972 Change. (But keep in mind that if the financing statement is not an appropriate method of perfection as to a type of proceeds, or is filed in the wrong place as to that type of proceeds, it will not constitute perfection; see the promissory-note-as-collateral example *supra*, p. 104.)

3. **Conflict between holder of proceeds interest and holder of direct accounts interest:** The proceeds of one secured party's collateral may be another secured party's original collateral. In particular, there may be a conflict between a security interest in the proceeds of, say, the debtor's inventory or equipment, and a security interest in *accounts*, if the inventory or equipment is sold on credit.

   a. **Discussed previously:** The resolution of this conflict is discussed in detail *supra*, p. 81. In brief, a purchase money lender against inventory will keep his special purchase-money priority as to the proceeds of the sale of that inventory only if the debtor receives *cash* (i.e., payment before or at the moment of delivery); if the debtor sells on credit, the purchase-money inventory financier will get no special priority as against the financier of accounts. Instead, the conflict will be governed by §9-312(5), and whoever either filed or perfected first will generally prevail. A purchase money lender against *non-inventory* will keep his special priority in the proceeds even if the original collateral is sold on credit, and even as against a direct financier of accounts. (However, this non-inventory purchase money lender must perfect within ten days of the time the debtor takes possession of the collateral.)

4. Illustrations: The following Hypotheticals illustrate some of the workings of the "proceeds" provisions of Article 9.

> **Hypothetical 1:** Appliance Manufacturer sold a number of dishwashers to Dealer on conditional sales contracts. It filed a proper financing statement. Dealer, who had permission to resell, sold one of these dishwashers on a conditional sales contract to Purchaser, for the latter's personal use. Dealer did not file a financing statement. Subsequently, Purchaser sold the dishwasher to Neighbor for the latter's personal use. Purchaser then defaulted. We will examine the rights of Appliance Manufacturer and Dealer.
>
> ***Appliance Manufacturer v. Purchaser:*** Because the sale to Purchaser was authorized, Purchaser took free of Appliance Manufacturer's interest under §9-306(2). Thus Appliance Manufacturer has no rights directly against Purchaser. It has, however, a security interest in the chattel paper which is the proceeds of Dealer's sale, which is perfected because of the original filing (since an interest in chattel paper may be perfected by filing.) Thus upon Dealer's default Appliance Manufacturer could eventually become the owner of the chattel paper. See *Appliance Manufacturer v. Dealer, infra*, p. 108.
>
> ***Dealer v. Purchaser:*** While the dishwasher was still in Purchaser's possession, Dealer had a valid security interest in it. In fact, since it was a purchase money security interest in consumer goods, it was perfected without filing under §9-302(1)(d). However, once the sale was made to Neighbor, Dealer lost his interest in the dishwasher (see *Dealer v. Neighbor*, below). However, Dealer still has an interest in the **proceeds** received by Purchaser. §9-306(2). Dealer's interest in the proceeds will continue perfected for 10 days after the payment to Purchaser; after that, assuming that the proceeds were money, Dealer will be perfected only if he somehow gets possession of the money (since an interest in money cannot be perfected by filing — §9-304(1), and since §9-306(3)(b) apparently protects identifiable cash proceeds if a financing statement is filed against the original collateral **before** the end of the 10-day period.)
>
> ***Dealer v. Neighbor:*** §9-307(2), which governs sales "by amateurs to amateurs," allows Neighbor to take free of Dealer's security interest in the dishwasher, since Dealer has not filed a financing statement covering the dishwasher.
>
> ***Appliance Manufacturer v. Neighbor:*** Since Purchaser took free of Appliance Manufacturer's interest (see *Appliance Manufacturer v. Purchaser* above) Neighbor receives the same clear title (at least with respect to

Appliance Manufacturer's interest) that Purchaser had. This result is reached by either §2-403 or by the common law "shelter" principle (*supra*, p. 74).

Appliance Manufacturer v. Dealer: Appliance Manufacturer has a security interest in the proceeds of the sale by Dealer to Purchaser. This proceeds interest is in chattel paper. Since an interest in chattel paper as original collateral could have been perfected by the filing of a financing statement, Appliance Manufacturer's financing statement will be sufficient to make the chattel paper proceeds interest also perfected. Thus if Dealer defaults, Appliance Manufacturer has the right under §9-502(1) to collect directly from Purchaser, the account debtor. However, since Purchaser has defaulted, this right is by itself of no consolation. But Appliance Manufacturer also presumably gets the right to sue Purchaser under its own name.

Hypothetical 2: Bank lends Ford Dealer the funds to acquire inventory under a written security agreement. The agreement provides for Bank to lend against specific cars as they are shipped by the manufacturer. As each individual car loan is made, Ford executes a chattel mortgage on it. Proceeds are covered both in the security agreement and in the financing statement which is filed. Consumer buys a car from Ford, signing a conditional sales contract covering the whole purchase price. Ford then sells the conditional sales contract to ABC Finance, which takes possession of the contract. Ford goes bankrupt. Bank and ABC each demands that Consumer make payments to it. We will look at the priority conflict, and also at how the losing party might have reversed the result.

Bank automatically gets a security interest in the proceeds of the disposition of inventory by Ford. Thus the chattel paper which Ford receives from Consumer constitutes proceeds, and Bank has a security interest in it.

However, §9-308 gives priority to ABC over Bank's proceeds interest in the chattel paper. §9-308 provides that "A purchaser of chattel paper . . . who gives new value and takes possession of it in the ordinary course of his business has priority over a security interest in the chattel paper . . . (b) which is claimed merely as proceeds of inventory subject to a security interest (§9-306) even though he knows that the specific paper . . . is subject to the security interest." Thus ABC takes free of Bank's interest even if it knew of Bank's security interest at the time it bought the chattel paper.

There are two things Bank could have done to prevent ABC from gaining priority. First of all, it could have taken possession of the chattel paper — §9-308 only applies to a purchaser who takes physical possession of the chattel paper. However, this would have been difficult for Bank to arrange for every individual car sale. Alternatively, Bank could have taken an interest in the chattel paper itself, and filed against it directly. This would have brought the case under §9-308(a), not (b), and would defeat ABC if it knew about Bank's security interest. (§9-308(a) protects a buyer only if he doesn't know about the security interest at the time he buys; §9-308(b) gives protection even though the buyer knows about the security interest.) Bank could then have stamped each conditional sales contract with a notation that this contract was covered by Bank's security interest; ABC would be charged with this knowledge.

VII. FUTURE ADVANCES

A. Generally: Suppose a secured party makes a security agreement with a debtor, and gives a loan under that agreement; the purpose of the agreement is to give the creditor security for the loan. Now suppose that subsequently, the secured party makes additional loans to the debtor. Are these loans also secured by the same collateral securing the first loan? Or are the parties required to make a new security agreement for every new loan? The answer is given in §9-204(3): "Obligations covered by a security agreement may include future advances or other value whether or not the advances or value are given pursuant to commitment." In other words, even if the secured party does not commit himself to make these future loans in the original security agreement, they are still covered when he does make them.

   1. Requirement that future advances be mentioned in agreement: The provision of §9-204(3) quoted above might indicate that future advances are covered whether or not the security agreement provides for them. However, Comment 5 to §9-204 states that "collateral may secure future as well as present advances when the security agreement so provides." This indicates, by negative implication, that future advances are covered only if the security agreement so provides. The matter is thus in doubt, and a prudent draftsman will always provide in the security agreement that future advances are to be covered. See Henson, 169.

B. Priority conflict with other security interest: One type of priority conflict which may involve future advances is between *two secured parties*. Typically, Secured Party A makes a loan and perfects by filing, Secured Party B makes a loan and perfects by filing and Secured Party A then makes a subsequent loan (either under the original security agreement or under a new one.)

1. **Future advances mentioned:** If Secured Party A's original security agreement explicitly mentioned future advances as being covered, there has never been any doubt that Secured Party A has priority even as to the second loan over Secured Party B. Under the present version of §9-312(5), this is a straightforward application of the rule that priority belongs to the person who either perfects or files first (since Secured Party A filed before Secured Party B either filed or perfected.)

2. **One-shot deal:** Where, however, the original security agreement was contemplated by the parties as being merely a *"one-shot deal"*, not a series of loans, the answer to the priority conflict has not always been so clear.

   a. **1962 Code ambiguous:** The 1962 Code did not furnish any explicit solution. Most courts held that even in this situation, Secured Party A prevails. But there were cases to the contrary; see, e.g., *Coin-O-Matic v. Rhode Island Hospital Trust Co.*, 3 U.C.C. Rep. Serv. 1112 (R.I. Super. Ct. 1966), holding that the second lender has priority over the first lender's unexpected subsequent advance. (The court noted that not only did the original security interest not contemplate future advances, but the financing statement also did not mention future advances. The court argued that a contrary ruling would unduly restrict the debtor's ability to borrow in the future from other lenders.)

   b. **Present Code resolution:** The present Code explicitly resolves this conflict in favor of Secured Party A (the original lender). §9-312(7) provides that "If future advances are made while a security interest is perfected by filing [or] the taking of possession . . . the security interest has the same priority for purposes of Subsection (5) with respect to the future advances as it does with respect to the first advance." Comment 7 to §9-312 makes it clear that the first lender's priority stems from the date of his original filing *even though the subsequent advance is not made under the original security agreement*, but is instead made under a new security agreement.

3. **Perfection by possession:** Observe that §9-312(7) also gives the first secured party priority as to his second advance if the means of perfection is *possession* rather than a filed financing statement (assuming that the possession continues up through the time of the subsequent advance.)

   Example: Debtor borrows money from Pawnbroker, and pledges his coin collection to Pawnbroker. Debtor then borrows from Bank, and Bank files a financing statement listing the coin collection. Debtor then goes back to Pawnbroker, and borrows additional money against the coin collection. Under §9-312(7), Pawnbroker has priority in the coin collection, even as to the second advance.

4. **Temporary perfection:** Suppose that the first secured party's interest is not perfected either by filing or possession, but by one of those "oddball" means of perfection (e.g., temporary perfection of an interest in instruments for twenty-one days under §9-304(4)). In this situation, §9-312(7) provides a special rule: a subsequent advance by the secured party has priority dating from the original (temporary) perfection only if the subsequent advance, or a "*commitment*" to make the advance, was made during the period of temporary perfection. If no such commitment was made during the temporary perfection, the subsequent advance made after the expiration of temporary perfection has a priority dating only from the time of the subsequent advance itself.

5. **Rationale:** The rationale for the priority given to the first secured party may be stated as follows: a party who has perfected a security interest either by filing or by possession has given notice to all others of his interest. Since it is quite common commercial practice for a lender or credit seller to make repeated advances, he should not have to worry about reperfecting his interest each time he makes a new advance. See Coogan, §3A.03, p. 199.

6. **Loan paid off:** Suppose the first lender has his loan *completely paid off*, but does not file a termination statement. If that lender makes a subsequent advance after an intervening secured party has lent and/or filed, who has priority? Nothing in §9-312(7) or anything else in Article 9 explicitly resolves this question. White and Summers argue that even in this situation, the first creditor should prevail, on the grounds that "the rationale behind §9-312(5)(a) and 9-312(7) is that once a lender has filed as to debtor's collateral, all subsequent lenders are on notice of first lender's claim. If second lender discovers first lender's filing, he can inquire of debtor and under 9-404(1), debtor can require first lender to file a termination statement in appropriate circumstances." See W&S, p. 1039, n. 15.

7. **No mention of future advances in financing statement:** There is apparently *no* requirement that the *financing statement mention that future advances are covered*. The Code nowhere explicitly imposes such a requirement. Also, the fact that the 1972 Code dropped the requirement that an interest in proceeds be explicitly claimed in the financing statement indicates that a similar policy should probably be followed with respect to claiming future advances.

C. Conflict with non-Article 9 interests: Where the conflict is between a secured party who has made a subsequent advance and a *non-Article*

9 interest, the equities are somewhat different. There are two common conflicts of this nature: (1) between the future advances secured party and a *lien creditor* who gets his lien between the original loan and the subsequent advance; and (2) between the secured party and a *subsequent purchaser*, who buys the collateral before the subsequent advance is made.

1. **Lien creditor:** The present Code explicitly deals with the rights of a *lien creditor* who obtains his lien between the time an original security interest arises, and the time when a later advance is made by that secured party.

   a. **§9-301(4):** This problem is dealt with by §9-301(4), which provides that "A person who becomes a lien creditor while a security interest is perfected takes subject to the security interest only to the extent that it secures advances made before he becomes a lien creditor or within forty-five days thereafter or made without knowledge of the lien or pursuant to a commitment entered into without knowledge of the lien."

   b. **What this means:** In other words, the post-lien advance, together with the advances made prior to the lien, comes ahead of the lien creditor if *any one* of the following three conditions is met:

      i. the post-lien advance is made within forty-five days after the lien came into existence;

      ii. the advance, even though it is made more than forty-five days after creation of the lien, was made without the secured party's having knowledge of the lien's existence; or

      iii. the post-lien advance was made pursuant to a *commitment* entered into by the secured party without knowledge of the lien.

      See Coogan, §3A.03, p. 202.

   c. **Lien holder should give notice:** Thus once the lien creditor has obtained his lien, he should pursue the following strategy: he should wait for the first forty-five days without giving any notice to the secured party. Then, at the end of the forty-five days he should notify the secured party of his lien, so that any subsequent advances made by the secured party will not squeeze out the lien creditor's priority.

   d. **Federal Tax Lien Act:** The forty-five day period was chosen to mesh with the Federal Tax Lien Act of 1966. The combination of the Federal Act and §9-301(4) assures that a security interest for an advance against certain types of collateral (defined in the Federal Act) made within forty-five days after a federal tax lien has been filed will have priority over that tax lien. See Coogan, §3A.03, p. 203.

e. **1962 Code does not resolve:** The 1962 Code does not explicitly resolve the rights of a lien creditor who gets his lien between the original perfection and the subsequent advance. (§9-301(4) was a completely new provision added in the 1972 Code.)

2. **Purchasers of collateral:** Suppose that the intervening non-Code interest is a *purchaser*, rather than a lien creditor. Does the purchaser who buys the collateral between the time of the first advance and the later one take free of the later one?

   a. **Ordinary course purchaser:** If the purchaser buys *in ordinary course of business*, recall that he takes prior to even the earlier-perfected security interest, under §9-307(1)). *A fortiori*, he will take prior to the subsequent advance; no special provision is needed to give him this right.

   b. **Non-ordinary course buyer:** But if the buyer is a *non-ordinary course* purchaser, he cannot rely on §9-307(1). However, §9-307(3) has been added to the 1972 Code; it provides that "A buyer other than a buyer in ordinary course of business . . . takes free of a security interest to the extent that it secures future advances made after the secured party acquires knowledge of the purchase, or more than forty-five days after the purchase, whichever first occurs, unless made pursuant to a commitment entered into without knowledge of the purchase and before the expiration of the forty-five day period."

      i. **What this means:** This section thus gives substantially less protection to the secured party than does the corresponding section involving rights of an intervening lien creditor (discussed *supra*). The secured party must normally meet two requirements in order to have his subsequent advance take priority against the non-ordinary course purchaser: (1) the secured party must not have known about the sale at the time he made the advance; and (2) less than forty-five days must have passed since the sale. (Thus the secured creditor is placed on the burden of ascertaining whether, as of forty-five days previously, the debtor still owned the collateral.) However, the advance will have priority if the secured party shows that it was made pursuant to a *commitment*, and the commitment was made during the forty-five day period without knowledge of the purchase. See Coogan, §3A.03, p. 201.

VIII. SUBROGATION

A. Generally: Article 9 regulates a number of conflicts between the interests of a secured party and that of a non-secured party. For example, §9-301(1)(b) governs the rights of a lien creditor as against those of an unperfected security interest; §9-307(1) and (2) govern the rights of certain purchasers of the collateral, etc. There has been great dispute about whether the rights of one particular interest — a *surety* — are governed by the Code.

   1. Where issue arises: The issue has most frequently arisen in the context of construction contracts. An owner of real estate will usually, before giving a contractor a contract to work on the property, require that the latter post a performance bond underwritten by a surety. Such a bond provides that if the contractor defaults, the surety will complete the contract, and will pay off laborers and suppliers of materials. If the surety does in fact have to step in and finish the contract, it is entitled, under the equitable doctrine of *subrogation*, to the money that the owner would have had to pay the contractor if the latter had not defaulted.

      a. Conflict: Complications arise, however, if the contractor has granted a security interest in its "contract rights," that is, in its right to payment when the building contract is performed. Thus, the contractor's secured party and the surety will be competing for the same funds owed by the owner, if the contractor defaults and the surety completes performance. Does Article 9 resolve this conflict? The trend is now for courts to hold that "since the surety's claim to these monies is not based on a security interest in them, Article 9 does not apply." W&S, 889.

B. *National Shawmut* case: One case which held that a conflict between a surety and the contractor's secured party is not governed by Article 9 is *National Shawmut Bank v. New Amsterdam Casualty Co.*, 411 F.2d 843 (1st Cir. 1969). In that case, the collateral over which the secured party (Shawmut Bank) and the surety (Amsterdam) were in conflict was money due from the owner (the U.S.) for work done by the contractor *prior* to default, but never paid.

   1. Holding: The court first held that the surety's right to payment by the owner was not an Article 9 security interest. The court advanced several reasons for this:

      a. §9-102(2) applies only to those security interests "created by contract" — here, "the real security is not the assignment of accounts receivable — which could be, failing the completion of performance, set off by the government — but the eventual right to be in the shoes of the government upon job completion.

This is not 'created by contract' but rather by the status, resulting from a contract, inhering in a surety, quite independently of the express terms of the contract."

  i. The court emphasized that the surety was subrogated not only to the contractor's right to receive payment from the owner, but also to the owner's rights, one of which was the right to subtract from payment for work already done its own cost of having to complete it. Thus once the surety had completed, it was subrogated to the rights the owner would have had to subtract its costs of completion from the progress payments owed but not paid. The surety therefore obtained by equitable principles the right to the money earned by the contractor before default but not paid to the latter. This right was not a right "created by contract" but rather one created by surety law.

 b. "Security interest" is defined in §1-201(37) (as it stood under the 1962 Code) to include a buyer of accounts or contract rights. The court held that the surety's right to finish the job and thus to minimize its own losses is neither a contract right nor an account. Furthermore, the court held, this right is not "goods, documents, instruments, general intangibles [or] chattel paper", or any of the other kinds of collateral listed in §9-102(2). Thus, this right to complete performance and be subrogated was not Article 9 collateral, and there could not be an Article 9 security interest in it.

 c. In the Code as originally drafted, a provision would have made "a security interest which secures an obligation to reimburse a surety" subordinate to a later lender who perfects. The court cited the rejection of this proposed provision as an indication that a surety's right to subrogation was not a "security interest" under the Code.

2. Equitable argument rejected: In addition to holding that the surety's right of subrogation was not displaced by the Code, the court also held that the Bank did not have any claim in equity superior to the surety's right of subrogation. If, prior to default, the contractor had assigned progress payments to the Bank, and the Bank had received payment, the Bank would not under equitable principles have been divested by the surety. But once the surety stepped in and completed performance, it gained superior equitable right to progress payments that had never been made by the owner. If the owner had had to complete performance itself, it would have had the right to apply to its own expenses of completion the progress payments which the contractor had earned prior to default and not received. The surety, by completing, became subrogated to this right of setoff of the government; the surety thus gained the right to apply against its own completion the progress payments earned by the contractor.

FIXTURES

I. INTRODUCTION

A. Nature of a "fixture": Article 9 in general deals only with security interests in *personal property*, not real property. There is, however, one class of items which is neither wholly personal nor wholly real; this is the category commonly called "fixtures".

1. **What is a "fixture":** A fixture is in general an item which is sufficiently incorporated into, or attached to, real estate that holders of interests in the real estate can claim at least some interest in that item. For instance, if the owner of a house installs a built-in dish washer, or a new furnace, the bank which holds the mortgage on the house can probably claim (under state non-UCC law) an interest in the dish washer or furnace. However, state law varies enormously on exactly what constitutes a fixture, and no state has a crystal-clear test.

2. **Article 9 does not define:** Article 9's fixtures section (§9-313) does not attempt to give a general definition of "fixture". Instead, it leaves this to local state non-UCC law. The way it does this is by providing that "goods are 'fixtures' when they become so related to particular real estate that an interest in them arises under real estate law." To put it another way, the item is a fixture under local law if a deed for the real estate would be sufficient to pass title to the item.

   a. **Ordinary building materials:** The text of §9-313 does disclose one category which *cannot* be considered a fixture: §9-313(2) states that "No security interest exists under this Article in *ordinary building materials* incorporated into an improvement on land." Thus bricks, mortar, lumber, etc. used in the construction of a structure will always be pure real estate interests, and cannot give rise to an Article 9 fixture interest.

3. **How states define fixture:** The states are not at all in agreement on what constitutes a fixture. However, most states attach importance to one or both of the following factors: (1) what the parties *intended* (e.g., as between landlord and tenant, whether the parties intended that the tenant would be allowed to remove the item at the end of the lease term); and (2) how difficult and destructive of the realty it would be to remove the item; the more difficult and destructive, the more likely the item is to be found to be a fixture. Thus an air conditioner which could easily be removed from a window is less likely to be found to be a fixture than an elevator which

could only be removed by taking off the roof and performing complex dismantling procedures.

    a. Mobile home may be fixture: Some *mobile homes* are fixtures. Most mobile homes are placed on leased land and remain personal property rather than a fixture. Occasionally, however, a mobile home is attached to the real estate to such a degree as to become an integral part of the site and hence a fixture. See Official Comment to §9-313. This is especially likely where the owner of the home also owns the underlying land.

        Example: Debtor purchases a mobile home from X and gives X a security interest in it. X assigns its security interest to Endicott, who files a financing statement pursuant to §9-302(1)(d) (which governs perfection of interests in motor vehicles, and which has sometimes been held to apply to mobile homes.) Debtor purchases from Wemco the land on which the home is placed, and gives back to Wemco a purchase money mortgage. In constructing the home, Debtor has a crawl space dug, footings installed and cinder block cemented to the footings to hold the home. The building's two sections are bolted together and covered with siding. The house appears to be a normal ranch-style home. The issue is whether the home is a chattel to which the ordinary motor-vehicle filing requirements of §9-302(1)(d) apply, or a fixture attached to real property and thus covered by §9-313.

        Held, the home is a fixture because of its very tight annexation to the land. To move the house it would be necessary to "dismantle it, separate it into two parts, remove part of the roofing and remove five to six feet of the center strips of shingles at either end of the home." (Therefore, Wemco has a perfected security interest in the home, and Endicott's interest is unperfected.) *In re Fink*, 4 B.R. 741 (B.Ct. W.D.N.Y. 1980).

B. Scope of Article 9 fixture provision: §9-313, the only provision of Article 9 that deals significantly with fixtures, regulates only one type of priority conflict: a conflict between the holder of an Article 9 security interest in the fixture *as a chattel*, and the holder of an interest in the *real estate* to which the fixture is affixed.

    1. Two personal property interests: Thus if two parties each claimed an Article 9 security interest in a fixture, the conflict would not be regulated by §9-313 at all; instead, it would fall under §9-312.

    2. Two real estate interests: Conversely, if a dispute arose between two real estate interests (e.g., the owner of the real estate, and the mortgagee), again this conflict would not be regulated by §9-313.

(Instead, it would be resolved under local real estate law).

3. **Purchase money interest:** In the substantial majority of situations where §9-313 applies, the conflict will be between the holder of a *purchase money security interest* in an item, and the holder of a real estate interest in that item (generally a secured party, i.e., a mortgagee).

> **Example:** Homeowner buys a new wall oven from Sears Roebuck, which a contractor builds into the wall of Homeowner's house. The oven is bought under a conditional sales contract which gives Sears a security interest in the oven. A conflict between Sears and the holder of a mortgage on Homeowner's house would be resolved by §9-313.

C. **Protection of real estate searchers:** The draftsmen of the 1972 Code felt that it would be desirable to give the personal property secured party priority over the real estate interest in at least some circumstances. Yet if this priority was to exist, some way had to be found to let the holders of real estate interests learn about the superior Article 9 interest. An ordinary Article 9 filing would not be sufficient for this purpose, since a real estate lender or purchaser does not typically check the Article 9 filing records (which will often be located centrally, in the secretary of state's office, rather than at the county level where most real estate searching is done.)

1. **"Fixture filing" solution:** Therefore, the draftsmen decided upon a special type of filing known as a *"fixture filing"*. A "fixture filing" is defined in §9-313(1)(b) as "the filing in the office where a mortgage on the real estate would be filed or recorded of a financing statement covering goods which are or are to become fixtures. . . ." This fixture filing must meet the requirements of §9-402(5); thus it must give the following information:

   a. a *description of the real estate* (but not a full metes-and-bounds description of the sort required for, say, a deed or mortgage);

   b. a recital that the financing statement is to be filed in the real estate records;

   c. a recital that goods which are or are to become fixtures are covered; and

   d. the name of the *record owner*, if the debtor has no interest of record. (Then, the real estate records office can index the financing statement not only under the debtor's name, but under the name of the owner of record. This will permit the real estate searcher to discover the document, even if he does not know the debtor's name. See §9-403(7).)

2. **Significance of "fixture filing":** Under the 1962 Code, an Article 9 secured party who wished to perfect an interest in a fixture had no ability to select those parties he wished the interest to be good against: he either perfected properly (in the manner required for a fixture), in which case his interest was good against both certain real estate interests and against other Article 9 interests, or he did not perfect in this manner (in which case his interest was not good against either Article 9 interests or real estate interests.) But the present version of §9-313 gives the Article 9 secured party a *choice*: (1) if he wishes his interest to be good against certain real estate interests, he must (in most cases) make the "fixture filing" described above; but (2) if his only concern is to make the interest good against other Article 9 interests, or against subsequent holders of liens on the property, and he is not worried about protection against subsequent purchasers of the real estate, he need only perfect under *any method* permitted by Article 9 (e.g., a regular Article 9 filing.)

a. **Rationale:** The rationale for this choice is that a fixture filing should be necessary for priority only over those persons who normally search the real estate records. Typically, this category will consist only of purchasers of the real estate, or those lending against it. Another Article 9 secured party, or a person acquiring a lien on the real estate, will not rely on the real estate records; therefore, regular Article 9 perfection should be sufficient as against such a person. See Coogan, §3A.02, pp. 177-78.

Example: Manufacturer sells a boiler to Homeowner, and takes a purchase money security interest to secure the purchase price. If Manufacturer wishes to make sure that its interest will have priority over the holder of the mortgage on Homeowner's house, Manufacturer will have to make a fixture filing (and will have to do so either before the furnace is installed or within ten days thereafter; see *infra*). But if Manufacturer only wants to protect itself against other Article 9 interests (e.g., a bank which might take a security interest in all of Homeowner's personal property), or against the holder of a lien on Homeowner's house, all that is required is ordinary Article 9 perfection. No filing is even necessary for such perfection, since Manufacturer is holding a purchase money security interest in consumer goods (see *supra*, p. 22).

II. PRIORITY RULES FOR FIXTURES

A. **Effect of non-purchase money fixture filing:** We now come to priorities which one achieves by making a fixture filing. First, suppose that the Article 9 lender is *not* holding a purchase money security interest.

1. **Conditions:** If he makes a fixture filing, §9-313(4)(b) provides that he will have priority over the holder of an encumbrance or ownership interest in the real estate if the following conditions are met:

   a. the perfection is made by the fixture filing ***before the real estate encumbrancer or owner records***;

   b. the Article 9 interest has priority over any interest of a ***predecessor in title*** of the real estate encumbrancer or owner; and

   c. the debtor has either an ***interest of record*** in the real estate, or is in possession of the real estate. (Thus if the debtor is a short-term tenant, the Article 9 party can take priority over a later-recorded real estate interest, since the tenant is in possession. But if the Article 9 debtor were merely, say, a contractor doing work on the premises, the person making a loan to the contractor secured by an Article 9 interest in the fixture would not have priority, since the contractor is neither in possession nor the holder of a record interest in the property.)

2. **Real estate interest already on record:** §9-313(4)(b) thus states in essence the "first-in-time" rule, similar to §9-312(5)'s rule where the conflict is between two Article 9 interests. This first-in-time rule means that if the real estate interest is ***already on record*** at the time the Article 9 interest arises, the Article 9 interest will lose (assuming that it is a non-purchase money interest).

   > **Example:** Bank holds a recorded mortgage on Homeowner's house. Finance Co., in return for a general loan to Homeowner, takes a security interest in all of Homeowner's personal possessions and fixtures. Finance Co. also makes a fixture filing. As to Homeowner's fixtures (e.g., his built-in dishwasher and built-in range, his furnace, etc.) Bank, not Finance Co., will have priority since it was first to record. (But an exception is given by §9-313(4)(c) if the fixtures are "readily removable replacements of domestic applicances which are consumer goods. . . ." See *infra*, p. 122).

B. **Purchase-money interest:** Just as in the case of a conflict between two Article 9 interests, the Article 9 ***purchase money*** financier of a fixture is given special rights.

   1. **Conditions:** Under §9-313(4)(a), the holder of a purchase money security interest in a fixture takes prior to the owner of a real estate interest in the property if:

      a. the security interest is perfected by a fixture filing ***before the goods become fixtures*** or ***within ten days thereafter***; and

      b. the debtor has an interest of record in the real estate or is in possession of it; and

   c. the real estate interest arose ***before the goods became fixtures***. (If the real estate interest arose after the Article 9 interest was perfected, the regular "first in time" rule of §9-314(4)(b) applies, so that the Article 9 interest wins anyway. But if a real estate interest arises between the time the goods become fixtures, which happens when they are affixed to the real estate, and the time the fixture filing is made — i.e., during the ten-day "grace period" — the real estate interest wins. See Coogan, §3A.02, p. 179.)

      Example: Bank holds a mortgage on Homeowner's house. Homeowner wishes to buy a new furnace, and borrows money for that purpose from Finance Co., which takes a security interest in the furnace. Finance Co. makes a fixture filing before the furnace is installed. Finance Co. will have priority in the furnace (and will therefore be allowed to remove it in the event of default) over Bank's mortgage. This would also be true if Finance Co. filed less than ten days after the furnace was installed.

C. "Readily removable" fixtures: Because of the vagueness (and state-to-state variation) in the definition of "fixture", an Article 9 secured party will not always know whether an item he is financing will be treated as a fixture. If he wishes the interest to be good against most real estate interests, he will have to make a "fixture filing" (see *supra*, p. 106), and he may have to make a separate Article 9 filing to protect himself against other Article 9 secured parties. However, §9-313(4)(c) (which has no counterpart under the 1962 Code) offers some relief as to a certain class of items: under that section, the Article 9 secured party has priority over a conflicting real estate interest if "the fixtures are ***readily removable factory or office machines***, or ***readily removable replacements of domestic appliances which are consumer goods***, and before the goods become fixtures the security interest is perfected by ***any method*** permitted by this Article."

   1. What this means: This means that as to certain factory and office machines, and certain replacement domestic appliances, the Article 9 secured party ***does not have to make a fixture filing***. Instead, he must merely perfect by any method allowed by Article 9 (usually, the filing of a financing statement). In fact, in the case of readily removable replacements of domestic appliances which are consumer goods, ***generally no filing will be necessary*** (since the Article 9 secured party's interest will almost always be a purchase money interest, and no Article 9 filing is necessary for perfection of such a purchase money security interest in consumer goods; see *supra*, p. 22).

2. **What "readily removable" means:** §9-313 gives no help in determining what "readily removable" means. Certainly such "loose" equipment as typewriters, photocopiers and computers are included. See W&S, p. 1060. But it is not clear whether heavier industrial machinery (e.g., a hydraulic lift in a gas station) would be included.

3. **Home appliances:** Not all domestic appliances that are easily removable fall within the special provision of §9-313(4)(c). Only those appliances which are *replacements* are covered. Thus if Developer sells homes with dishwashers, ovens, etc. already built in, the holders of Article 9 security interests in those appliances must make a fixture filing if they are to have priority over real estate interests. But then, if the purchaser of the house replaces, say, the dishwasher, the seller or financier of the new dishwasher does not need to make any filing at all (since his interest is a purchase money interest in consumer goods.)

   Note: Observe that the requirement that the Article 9 security interest attach before the goods become affixed means that the interest will almost always be a purchase money interest. (A non-purchase money interest will generally attach only after the goods have been purchased and installed.)

D. **Construction mortgages:** One type of real estate interest is given special protection under §9-313. That is the *construction mortgage*. The construction mortgagee is the lender (typically a bank) which advances the money needed by the builder to carry out the construction itself. §9-313(6) gives this construction mortgagee one special priority which other real estate interests do not have: *he takes prior to certain subsequently-recorded Article 9 purchase-money security interests.*

   Example: Bank finances the construction of a small residential development by Developer; in return, it takes a construction mortgage. (That is, the mortgage is short-term, and is to be repaid with the proceeds of a permanent financing once the buildings have been built.) Shortly after Bank files its real estate mortgage, Developer buys 36 built-in dishwashers from Manufacturer, which takes an Article 9 security interest to secure the purchase price. Manufacturer makes a fixture filing before Developer installs the dishwashers. Bank, not Manufacturer, will have priority in the dishwashers because of its special status as construction mortgagee under §9-313(6). (If, on the other hand, Bank had been a non-construction mortgagee, it would have lost to Manufacturer even if Bank had filed first; this is because of the priority given to Article 9 purchase money secured parties against previously-filed real estate interests; see §9-313(4)(a).)

1. **No other interest affected:** §9-313(6) operates to give a construction mortgagee priority over a purchase money secured party only by cancelling the effect of §9-313(4)(a) (the section giving a purchase money secured party priority over certain previously-recorded interests.) If there is any other section which would give priority to the purchase money interest, that section will remain in effect as to the construction mortgagee.

   a. **"Readily removable" or waiver:** Thus if the fixtures are "readily removable" factory or office machines, or readily removable replacements of domestic appliances (both covered by §9-313(4)(c)), the purchase money secured party who has perfected under Article 9 gets priority over the construction mortgagee. Thus in the above example, if the dishwashers were replacement models rather than original equipment, Manufacturer would prevail even against Bank's construction mortgage. Similarly, if the debtor has a right to remove the goods as against the mortgagee (see §9-313(5)(b), discussed *infra*, p. 125) the construction mortgagee will lose.

   b. **Mortgagee's successor:** The *successor* of the construction mortgagee (i.e., the holder of a permanent mortgage on the property) also obtains this priority; but the priority only applies if the goods became fixtures *before the construction was completed*. Thus an Article 9 purchase money lender or credit seller should wait until the construction has been completed before making the payment or delivery that will result in installation of the fixture; he is thus insured of priority even over a construction mortgagee or such a mortgagee's successor.

E. **Fixture interest vs. lien creditor:** §9-313(4)(d) makes an Article 9 interest superior to a *"lien on the real estate* obtained by legal or equitable proceedings after the secured interest was perfected by any method permitted by [Article 9]." Thus the Article 9 interest is superior to a subsequent lien creditor even though the Article 9 claimant has not made a fixture filing (but has instead made, say, an ordinary Article 9 filing or has perfected without filing where this is permitted, as in the case of a purchase money interest in consumer goods.)

   1. **Effect in bankruptcy:** This provision has an important effect in *bankruptcy*. As is discussed *infra*, p. 132, the trustee's principal weapon for defeating an Article 9 security interest is by assuming the status of a lien creditor as of the time of bankruptcy; this permits the trustee to invalidate any interest not perfected as of the date of bankruptcy. What §9-313(4)(d) does is to prevent the trustee's lien-creditor status from being superior to an Article 9 fixture interest, provided that that interest was perfected (even if only

by Article 9 means, rather than by a special "fixture filing") prior to bankruptcy.

   a. Rationale: The Code draftsmen felt that a lien creditor does not typically rely on the state of the real estate records. Therefore, there was no reason to make the Article 9 claimant file a special fixture filing in order to have priority over that lien creditor (or over the bankruptcy trustee standing in his shoes). See W&S, p. 1061.

F. Waiver and tenant's rights: There are two other important crcumstances in which the Article 9 interest will have priority over a real estate interest. These situations, both of which apply *whether or not the Article 9 interest is perfected*, are stated by §9-313(5):

   1. Consent: First, the real estate interest (either mortgagee or owner) loses his priority if he has *consented in writing* to the security interest, or has *disclaimed any interest* in the goods as fixtures. §9-313(5)(a)). Thus in order to make the real estate interest as a whole more valuable, a bank which held a mortgage on property might well consent to give priority in certain fixtures to a new lender (e.g., a finance company specializing in home improvement loans).

   2. Tenant's rights: Second, the real estate interest is subordinate to the Article 9 claimant if "the *debtor* has a *right to remove* the goods as against the [real estate interest.]" §9-313(5)(b).

   > **Example:** Tenant's lease with Landlord provides that Tenant shall have the right to remove, at the end of the lease term, any air conditioners or other fixtures which may be readily removed without damage to the real estate. Finance Co., in return for a general loan to Tenant, takes a security interest in all of Tenant's personal property. If Tenant defaults, Finance Co. may remove the air conditioners notwithstanding Landlord's interest in the real estate. That is, under §9-313(3)(a), Finance Co. stands in Tenant's shoes, and may exercise Tenant's right to remove the goods as against Landlord. (But Finance Co. will have to pay for any damage caused to the real estate as a result of the removal; see *infra*, p. 126).

III. REMOVAL ON DEFAULT

A. Right to remove on default: If the debtor defaults, the Article 9 secured party will generally wish to exercise his self-help right of *repossession* (see *infra*, p. 128). Under the 1962 Code and prior law, his right to do so was unclear; many courts held that he could not do this if the real estate would be worth materially less without the fixture (even though the structure might not be physically damaged by the removal). But the present Code gives the Article 9 claimant a substantial right of removal upon his debtor's default.

1. **Secured creditor with priority:** If the Article 9 secured party has priority (under the rules discussed above) over *all persons* holding ownership or encumbrance interests in the real estate, he has the right to *remove his collateral* from the real estate upon the debtor's default. §9-313(8).

   a. *Pay for injury:* However, the secured party must *reimburse* any mortgagee, lien creditor, or owner, except for the debtor, for the *cost of repairing any physical injury to the premises*. (But the secured party is not liable for any "diminution in value of the real estate caused by the absence of the goods removed. . . ." §9-313(8).) Thus the secured party might have to pay for a hole caused by removing, say, a built-in dishwasher, but he would not have to pay for the amount by which the apartment or house was worth less because of the fact that it had no dishwasher.

   b. *Post bond:* Also, anyone who is entitled to reimbursement for physical damage caused by removal may require the secured party to give *adequate security* against this reimbursement obligation. Thus the secured party referred to in the previous paragraph might have to post a $100 bond as security against any hole or other physical damage which might be caused by removal of the dishwasher.

2. **Real estate interest has priority:** If a person holding a real estate interest (either a mortgagee, owner or lien creditor) has priority over the Article 9 claimant, the Article 9 claimant *may not repossess* without that prior party's permission.

   Example: Bank issues a construction mortgage on a house to be built by Developer. Developer buys built-in ranges from Manufacturer, in which Manufacturer takes a security interest which is filed as a fixture. Developer defaults in paying Manufacturer. Because Bank has priority over Manufacturer under §9-313(6), Manufacturer may not repossess the ranges without Bank's permission. Thus its only way to realize on its security is to hope that Bank will foreclose on its construction mortgage, and that Bank will be able to satisfy its entire debt out of the proceeds of the real estate apart from the ranges. See W&S, p. 1064.

BANKRUPTCY

I. GENERAL SCOPE

A. The trustee and the secured party: When a debtor goes into bankruptcy, the recently-enacted **Bankruptcy Code of 1978** provides for the appointment of a trustee to represent the unsecured creditors. His job is to marshal the debtor's assets so that these creditors can obtain the largest possible percentage of their claims in the bankruptcy distribution.

  1. Trustee's powers: The Bankruptcy Code gives the trustee a number of powers to aid him in marshalling the debtor's assets. First, he takes title to all of the debtor's property, and may assert any defenses which would have been available to the debtor. (§541). Furthermore, he may *stay* the secured party from repossessing the collateral (§362); he may attack an unperfected security interest by using his status as a "hypothetical lien creditor" (§544 (a)); he may assert the rights of an actual unsecured creditor under state law (§544(b)); he may avoid security interests which are defined as "fraudulent" by the Bankruptcy Code (§548); and he may set aside "preferential transfers", including certain security interests (§547).

  2. Security interest valid: However, the general rule is that a security interest which is created more than *three months before* the debtor's bankruptcy, and which is *promptly perfected*, cannot be set aside by the trustee. The secured party is therefore (eventually) allowed to either repossess the collateral himself, or to take the proceeds from the bankruptcy court's sale of the collateral.

B. Scope of discussion: This chapter begins by discussing the way in which the filing of a bankruptcy petition acts as a "stay" (delay) of a secured party's right to repossess the collateral. Then, the discussion shifts to treatment of the various ways in which the trustee may overturn the security interest, relegating the secured party to unsecured status and making the collateral available as part of the general "pot" for all unsecured creditors.

C. New Code vs. old Act: The Bankruptcy Code of 1978 was the first major recodification of federal bankruptcy law since the Bankruptcy Act of 1898, last substantially amended in 1938. Many of the most significant changes relate to bankruptcy procedures, and will not concern us very much here. However, some important changes, and quite a number of clarifications, have been made in the area of secured creditors' rights in bankruptcy. In this chapter, we will concentrate upon the 1978 Code (which we call the "new Code"), rather than on the 1938 Act (the "old

Act"). The new Code applies to any bankruptcy proceeding commenced after October 1, 1979. Coogan, §9C.01[1].

D. **Reorganizations and wage earners' plans:** If the debtor has absolutely no chance to regain his solvency, the proceeding will be one in "straight bankruptcy", falling under Chapter 7 of the Bankruptcy Code. In this event, a trustee is appointed to represent the bankrupt, and it is the trustee who asserts the powers of avoidance discussed in this chapter. But the avoidance powers may also come into play in two other types of bankruptcy proceedings.

   1. **Reorganization:** First, a business organization which has some chance of regaining solvency may file a petition for *reorganization* under Chapter 11 of the Code. In a reorganization proceeding, the debtor proposes a plan for gradually paying off, either in whole or in part, his creditors.

   2. **Wage earner:** Secondly, a "wage earner", i.e., a person with a job and a regular salary, may file for a plan of arrangement under Chapter 13 of the Code, whereby he can gradually pay off his creditors wholly or partly, without giving up all of his assets.

   3. **Effect on secured party:** The secured party's security interest in property of a debtor in reorganization, or in that of a wage earner in a Chapter 13 proceeding, may be affected the same way as in a straight bankruptcy. §103(a).

II. SECURED CREDITOR'S RIGHT TO REPOSSESS

A. **Desire to repossess promptly:** If the debtor files a bankruptcy petition, he is probably already in default under his various security agreements, or soon will be. Therefore, the secured party would like to be able to repossess the collateral promptly, using self-help repossession (*infra*, p. 158). However, a key feature of the Bankruptcy Code is that it *prevents* him from doing this. Under the *"automatic stay"* provision of §362, the filing of a bankruptcy petition stops a secured creditor from *repossessing*, perfecting, taking judicial action to foreclose, or virtually any other collection action.

   1. **Previously repossessed property:** Furthermore, even if the secured party had repossessed the property *prior to the filing* of the petition, the automatic stay will prevent him from disposing of the property. W&S, p. 1020. Also, he will probably be required to return the property to the trustee.

B. **Length of stay:** This automatic stay continues, in essence, for the entire bankruptcy proceeding, unless the judge orders otherwise. §362(c). But the secured party is free to apply to the court for relief from the stay. Generally, the secured party, in order to obtain relief from the stay, will have to show that either:

1. **Adequate protection for secured party:** A lifting of the stay is necessary to give the secured party "*adequate protection*" of his interest in the property (e.g., the value of the collateral is depreciating rapidly, and must be sold promptly if the secured party is to be made whole); or

2. **No equity:** The debtor has *no equity* in the collateral *and* the property is "not necessary to an effective reorganization." (Thus even if the debtor's debt was greater than the value of the collateral, the secured party could not get the stay lifted under this provision if the collateral was vital to an effective reorganization. This might be the case if it were, for instance, a machine used to produce all of the debtor's inventory.) See §362(d)(1) and (2).

C. **Debtor may use collateral:** To make the secured party's life even more difficult, §363 of the Code allows a trustee (or the debtor-in-possession in a reorganization) to *use, sell, or lease* the collateral. For instance, a debtor-in-possession in a reorganization may sell inventory, even though a creditor may hold a perfected security interest in that inventory. W&S, p. 1021.

   1. **Exceptions:** However, there are some exceptions to protect the secured party.

      a. **Non-ordinary course transaction:** First, a transaction that is not in the "ordinary course of business" may only take place following notice to the secured party and a hearing; the judge can order steps to be taken to protect the secured party.

      b. **Sale:** Secondly, although the debtor's right to *use* the collateral in the ordinary course of his business is relatively unrestricted, he does not have the right to *sell it* in all circumstances; however, he may make the sale if it is for a price greater than the value of the secured party's interest. (Thus if Secured Party is owed a debt of $1,000, secured by a lien on a carload of dresses, the dresses may be sold in the ordinary course of business for $1,100; the secured party would presumably get a security interest in the proceeds.)

      c. **Cash collateral:** Finally, if the collateral is what the Bankruptcy Code defines as "cash collateral" (cash, negotiable instruments, or other highly liquid assets), the trustee or debtor may not even use, let alone sell or lease, the collateral unless the secured party approves or the court has so ordered. §363(c)(2).

III. TRUSTEE'S RIGHT TO DEBTOR'S PROPERTY

A. **Assets and defenses of debtor:** Under §541 of the Code, the debtor turns over to the trustee virtually all of his assets (except for certain exemptions set forth in §522). Thus the trustee succeeds to any *equity* which the debtor may have in the collateral (e.g., collateral worth $1,000, where the secured debt is only $700, leaving $300 of equity.) Equally importantly, the trustee succeeds to any *defenses* which the debtor may have against third parties, including secured parties. §541(e). Thus to the extent that the debtor would be able to defeat a particular security interest in whole or in part, so may the trustee.

> **Example:** Bank lends money to Debtor, which the parties intend to be secured by a security interest on Debtor's accounts receivable. Bank draws up a security agreement, but Debtor never signs it. Debtor goes into bankruptcy. Since the trustee succeeds to all defenses which might be raised by Debtor against third parties, Trustee can avoid Bank's security interest by claiming that it does not satisfy the Statute of Frauds provision of UCC §9-203 (*supra*, p. 11). If Debtor could raise a defense of unconscionability, fraud, mutual mistake, etc., the same defense could be used by Trustee. See W&S, p. 996.

IV. TRUSTEE'S USE OF ACTUAL CREDITOR'S RIGHTS (§544(b))

A. **Use of actual creditor's rights:** If the trustee can find an *actual creditor* of the bankrupt who could, under *state law*, avoid a particular security interest in the bankrupt's property, the trustee may *step into that creditor's shoes*. B.C., §544(b).

1. **Practical use:** If the reason an actual creditor could avoid the security interest is that, on the date the bankruptcy petition was filed, the security interest had not been perfected, the trustee will not use §544(b). Instead, he will use §544(a)'s "strongarm" clause, discussed *infra*, p. 132. The utility of §544(b) is in those cases where the secured party delayed in perfecting, but still managed to perfect before the bankruptcy petition was filed. In such a situation, if the trustee can find an actual creditor who would be able to defeat the security interest (under applicable state law), the trustee may do the same.

2. **Moore v. Bay still survives:** An old Supreme Court case, *Moore v. Bay*, 284 U.S. 4 (1931), holds that under the predecessor of B.C. §544(b) (§70(e) of the old Bankruptcy Act), the trustee may invalidate the *entire* security interest, even if the actual creditor's claim is much less than the debt owed to the secured party. §544(b) preserves the rule of *Moore v. Bay*; see W&S, p. 1019.

> **Example:** Secured Party is owed $10,000 by Debtor, secured by all of Debtor's inventory. Secured Party does not perfect its security interest promptly. Before the security interest is

perfected, Shoe Co. sells Debtor a $10 pair of shoes. Assume that under applicable state law, a creditor who extends credit during the "gap" between the creation of a security interest and its perfection takes priority over the security interest. Shortly thereafter, Secured Party perfects, and still later, Debtor goes bankrupt. Under §544(b) (and under the rule of *Moore v. Bay*), Trustee steps into the shoes of Shoe Co., and is able to invalidate not only the first $10 worth of Secured Party's interest, but the **entire interest**. See Coogan, §9C.06[4][d]. See also *In re Plonta*, 311 F.2d 44 (6th Cir. 1962), holding that the trustee may invalidate the entire security interest no matter how small the amount of the actual gap creditor's claim.

3. **Limited importance under UCC:** But §544(b) is of limited importance today. Prior to the adoption of the Uniform Commercial Code, many states had statutes which allowed any person who extended credit during the gap between creation of a security interest and its perfection to upset that security interest. It is upon such a statute that the above example is constructed. But under Article 9 of the UCC, in force everywhere except Louisiana, **such a "gap" creditor does not take priority over an earlier, but unperfected, security interest.** It is only a creditor who **obtains a judicial lien** prior to perfection of the security interest who takes priority over that security interest (see §9-301(1)(b)). Therefore, unless the trustee is lucky enough to find an actual creditor who obtained a judicial lien prior to the perfection of the security interest (a most unlikely happening), the trustee will have no one's shoes into which to step.

   a. **Few cases where applicable:** However, apart from a gap creditor who obtains a lien prior to perfection of the security interest, there are two or three other situations where the trustee may be able to use §544(b). First, if the transaction is **fraudulent** under state law, but not under the Bankruptcy Code's own fraudulent conveyance section (§548), the trustee may be able to step into the shoes of an actual defrauded creditor. (For instance, the state fraudulent conveyance statute might have a longer statute of limitations than B.C. §548's one year.) Secondly, an actual creditor might obtain the right to invalidate an interest under other articles of the UCC; for instance, a creditor might be able to gain priority over a transferee of bulk assets under Article 6. See W&S, pp. 1018-19.

   b. **Can't use rights of other secured creditor:** Suppose that between the time an initial security interest is created, and when it is perfected, a **second secured party** creates an interest *and perfects it*. This second secured party has priority over the first under UCC §9-312(5)(a). Can the trustee step into the shoes of this second secured party to invalidate the first party's interest? Under B.C. §544(b), the answer is clearly "*no*", since that section refers solely to "a creditor holding an *unsecured* claim. . . ." See W&S, p. 1019.

V. SECURITY INTEREST NOT PERFECTED ON DATE OF BANKRUPTCY (§544(a))

A. Lack of perfection at bankruptcy: If the student only remembers one rule about the effect of bankruptcy upon security interests, it should be this one: any security interest that is *unperfected* as of the moment the bankruptcy petition is filed (except for certain recently-created purchase money security interests) is *void as against the trustee*.

1. **Why this result occurs:** This result is the combined product of federal and state law. Under B.C. §544(a)(1), the trustee has the rights of "a creditor that extends credit to the debtor at the time of the commencement of the case, and that obtains, at such time . . . a judicial lien on all property [of the debtor] . . . *whether or not such a creditor exists.*" Thus the trustee obtains *lien creditor status as of the moment the petition is filed*.

2. **Effect of UCC:** What are the rights of a lien creditor? These rights are determined by state law, namely, UCC §9-301(1)(b). Under this section, an *unperfected* security interest is *subordinate* to the rights of "a person who *becomes a lien creditor before the security interest is perfected.*"

   > **Example:** Secured Party and Debtor sign a security agreement on March 1, giving Secured Party a security interest in certain of Debtor's equipment. On May 1, while Secured Party has still not filed a financing statement, Debtor files a bankruptcy petition. On May 15, Secured Party files a financing statement. Even if no lien creditor existed at any time, the trustee will gain the rights that a lien creditor *would have had* on May 1, if one had existed. Since a creditor who obtained a lien on May 1 would have been superior to Secured Party at that point (because Secured Party's interest was not yet perfected), the trustee is superior to Secured Party.

3. **Perfection just before bankruptcy:** Observe that §544(a) gives a trustee his lien creditor status *only as of the moment the petition is filed*. Thus if the secured party gets wind of the debtor's intention to file a bankruptcy petition, and the secured party manages to perfect *just moments before* the bankruptcy petition is filed, the trustee cannot use §544(a). (However, the delay in perfection may cause the security interest to constitute a preference

under B.C. §547, discussed *infra*, p. 134.)

4. **Derives from old B.A. §79(c):** §544(a), giving trustee lien creditor status, is commonly called the trustee's "*strong-arm*" clause, because of its independence of whether a lien creditor actually exists, and its broad reach. The section derives from §70(c) of the old Bankruptcy Act.

B. **Exceptions:** There are two important *exceptions* to the general principle that the trustee may invalidate any security interest unperfected as of the date of bankruptcy.

1. **Transfer of exempt property not voidable:** Certain property of the debtor is *exempted* from becoming part of the bankrupt estate, by B.C. §522. If the debtor has given a security interest in exempt property, the trustee may not reclaim this property for the benefit of general creditors even if the security interest was not perfected as of the date of bankruptcy.

2. **Post-bankruptcy grace period for purchase money interests:** Recall that under UCC §9-301(2), as long as the holder of a *purchase money* security interest files within ten days after the debtor takes possession of the collateral, the secured party has priority over a creditor who obtained a lien between the time the security interest attached and the time of filing. (See *supra*, p. 87). In a bankruptcy context, that means that a purchase money secured party *keeps his ten-day grace period*, even if a bankruptcy petition intercedes. (This result is made explicit by B.C. §546(b).)

    Example: Bank lends Businessman money to buy a new machine to be used for production. The security agreement is signed on June 1, but Businessman does not pay over the proceeds of the loan to the machine's seller until September 15, and does not take possession of the machine until November 1. Businessman files a bankruptcy petition on November 5. Bank files a financing statement on November 9. Even though the trustee in bankruptcy has lien creditor status as of November 5, he will not be able to upset Bank's security interest, since under UCC §9-301(2), Bank would prevail against a creditor who obtained a lien on November 5.

C. **Where perfection has lapsed:** Normally, §544(a) will be used where the security interest has never been perfected at all. But it may also be used where the perfection has *lapsed* prior to bankruptcy. For instance, where more than five years has passed since the original financing statement was filed, and no continuation statement has been filed, the trustee will be able to use §544(a). See UCC §9-403(2), discussed *supra*, p. 30.

D. Trustee's knowledge irrelevant: In states where the 1962 version of UCC §9-301(1)(b) is in effect (about half of the states; see *supra*, p. 2), a lien creditor takes prior to an earlier unperfected security interest only if the lien creditor became such without knowing about the security interest. However, any knowledge of the unperfected interest by either the trustee or by all creditors is made *irrelevant* by B.C. §544(a), and the trustee's ability to use §544(a) is unimpeded. (Where the 1972 version of §9-301(1)(b) is in effect, the knowledge of the lien creditor is made irrelevant even as a matter of state law.)

VI. DELAYED PERFECTION AS PREFERENCE (§547)

A. Striking down delayed perfection: If the security interest is unperfected as of the date of bankruptcy, the trustee can almost always strike it down under §544(a), as we have seen. If he can find an actual unsecured creditor who obtained a lien during the gap between creation of the security interest and its perfection, he can step into that unsecured creditor's shoes and void the security interest, under §544(b). But if the security interest is perfected just before bankruptcy, and no actual creditor got a lien in the gap, the trustee may still prevail. He does this by attacking the grant-and-perfection of the security interest as a *preferential transfer* under B.C. §547.

   1. Granting of security interest is transfer: A key aspect of the use of §547 to attack a security interest is that under B.C. 101(40), the mere *granting of a security interest* is itself considered to be a *transfer of property*. Thus whether or not the secured party has foreclosed on the collateral as of the date the bankruptcy petition is filed, the granting of a security interest constituted a transfer, which may or may not have been preferential. (As to the *time* at which the transfer is deemed to have occurred, see *infra*, p. 140.)

B. Policies behind preference rules: There are two quite distinct policy considerations behind giving the trustee the right to strike down preferential transfers.

   1. Equal treatment: First, at least where bankruptcy is imminent, the debtor should be required to give *equal treatment* to equally-situated creditors. In nearly all situations, the debtor himself has some advance knowledge that a petition (whether voluntary or involuntary) will be filed, and often is inclined to favor one creditor (perhaps a relative) over others. Such favoritism (whether it takes the form of making payment to that creditor, or of giving him a security interest) should not be allowed to stand. W&S, p. 999.

   2. Discouraging secret liens: Secondly, particularly in the case of security interests, there is a policy of *discouraging secret liens*. Just as the UCC penalizes a secured party who does not perfect (usually by a public filing), so the Bankruptcy Code manifests a policy in favor of perfection.

> **Example:** Both of these policies may be illustrated on the following facts: Bank makes an unsecured loan to Debtor on March 1. Finance Co. lends Debtor money on April 1, and takes a security interest in Debtor's equipment. In early June, Debtor realizes that he is hopelessly insolvent, and that he will ultimately end up in bankruptcy. Unlike Debtor's general trade creditors, Bank and Finance Co. keep in close contact with Debtor, and Debtor tells both in mid-June that he is thinking about bankruptcy. Bank pressures Debtor into giving it a security interest in inventory. Finance Co. rushes out and perfects its earlier security interest in the equipment. Debtor files a bankruptcy petition in early July.
>
> The trustee in bankruptcy will be able to knock down both Bank's and Finance Co.'s security interest. Invalidation of Bank's interest is justified on the grounds that Bank has received better treatment than other unsecured creditors during the time shortly before bankruptcy, since it has been converted to secured status. Invalidation of Finance Co.'s interest is justified on the grounds that Finance Co., kept its secured interest secret (by not perfecting), and other creditors who extended credit after April 1 may have been misled about the value of Debtor's unencumbered assets and the amount of his liabilities. (The actual mechanism by which each of these interests is struck down is discussed below.)

C. Requirements for striking down preference: B.C. §547(b) sets forth a number of elements which the trustee must show in order to invalidate any transfer as a voidable preference:

1. A *transfer*

2. of property of the debtor

3. to or for the benefit of a creditor

4. for or on account of an *antecedent debt* owed by the debtor *before the transfer was made*

5. made while the debtor was *insolvent*

6. made either: (i) within *90 days before the date the petition was filed*; or (ii) between 90 days and one year before the filing of the petition, if the creditor was an *"insider"* with reasonable cause to believe the debtor was insolvent; and

7. the transfer enables the creditor to receive more than he would have in a Chapter 7 (straight bankruptcy) liquidation had the transfer not been made.

Example: Consider the facts set forth in the previous example. Debtor clearly made a "transfer" to Bank when he gave it the security interest, and when he did so, he was insolvent. This security interest was granted less than 90 days before the bankruptcy petition was filed. Since Bank previously had unsecured status, then (assuming that Debtor's assets are not enough to pay off all creditors) Bank would end up getting a larger percentage of its debt satisfied than had it remained unsecured and been a general creditor in the straight bankruptcy proceeding. Therefore, all the requirements of §547(b) are met, and the trustee strikes down Bank's interest.

Much the same analysis goes for Finance Co.'s interest. One critical difference is that by §547(e)(1) and (2), the transfer of a security interest to Finance Co. is not deemed "made" until that transfer was *perfected*. Since perfection did not occur until less than ninety days before the petition was filed, three requirements for application of §547(b) are met which would not otherwise be: (1) the debt becomes an "antecedent" one, since antecedency is determined by when a transfer is "made" (i.e., when the security interest was "perfected"); (2) the transfer was "made" while Debtor was insolvent; and (3) the transfer was "made" less than 90 days before the petition was filed.

D. Discussion of elements: Some of the above elements are reasonably self-explanatory, but others need further discussion.

1. **"Transfer":** As noted, the giving of a security interest is clearly a transfer. As to the time the transfer is deemed made, see *infra*, p. 140.

2. **Exempt property of debtor:** The second requirement is that the property transferred be property "of the debtor". The old Bankruptcy Act required, in addition, that the property be *non-exempt*. But §547 of the new Act apparently includes exempt property as well. W&S, p. 1003. Thus if, shortly before bankruptcy, Debtor grants Bank a security interest in Debtor's car, worth $1,000 (an exempted asset up to a value of $1,200 under B.C. §522(d)(2)), and then makes payments to Bank of the $1,000 amount secured, all within ninety days of bankruptcy, the security interest could presumably be stricken (assuming that other requirements were met), and the payments therefore recovered.

3. **Antecedent debt:** §547(b) gives little help in determining what constitutes an *"antecedent debt"*, except to say that it is a debt "owed by the debtor before [the] transfer was made." But §547(c) contains a number of provisions which, in effect, prevent certain payments from being on account of antecedent debt.

a. **"Substantially contemporaneous"**: §547(c)(1) saves from being preferential a transfer which is intended by both parties to be a *"contemporaneous exchange"* for new value, if the transfer is *in fact* a *"substantially contemporaneous exchange"*.

> **Example:** Seller sells a stereo to Debtor. At the time Debtor takes the stereo, he gives Seller a non-certified check. Because the check is drawn on an out-of-state bank, it does not clear for seven days (and the proceeds are thus not deposited in Seller's account till then.) §547(c)(1) prevents the deposit of the proceeds in Seller's account from being a transfer on account of the antecedent debt, since both parties intended a cash sale, and the resulting transaction was almost the same thing.

> i. **Delay in filing:** But it is not clear whether §547(c)(1) will extend to a brief delay between the execution of a security agreement and its perfection. As discussed below, §547(e)(2)(A) gives the secured party a ten-day-grace period within which to file. But suppose that the gap is in fact, say, twelve days. May the secure party argue that the giving of the loan, the execution of the security agreement, and its perfection, were all as a simultaneous exchange, and that they amounted to a "substantially" contemporaneous exchange? White and Summers (p. 1006) suggest that the explicit grant of a ten-day-grace period manifests an intent of the draftsmen not to let a longer gap fall within §547(c)(1).

b. **Ordinary course payments:** Under §547(c)(2), a payment is not made on account of antecedent debt if it is in payment of a debt incurred in the *"ordinary course of business* or financial affairs of the debtor and the transferee"*, is made within *forty-five days* after the debt was incurred, the payment itself is in the ordinary course of business for both parties, and is made according to *"ordinary business terms"*. Thus the debtor may pay his usual bills in the usual manner, without these payments being attacked as preferences. This section will usually not have application to secured debts (since payment on the secured debt is not a preference, if the security interest itself is not a preference; see *infra*, p. 139.)

c. **Purchase money interests:** As discussed *infra*, p. 141, any secured party has a ten-day-grace period between the advancing of value and the perfecting of his security interest. But §547(c)(3) gives an additional grace period to a *purchase money* secured party. The purchase money security interest is deemed not made on account of an antecedent debt so long as it is perfected within ten days after the security interests "attaches" (which does not happen until, under UCC §9-203(1)(c), the debtor has "rights in the collateral".)

Example: Debtor wishes to acquire an expensive piece of custom-made machinery for his business. The manufacturer of the equipment will not begin work unless Debtor pays the full price in advance. Debtor goes to Bank for a loan to be used for this advance payment. Bank gives Debtor the money on June 1. Debtor gives Bank a purchase money security interest in the machine. Bank does not file right away. Debtor turns over the money to the manufacturer, who does not start work until July 1. On July 8, Bank files. The earliest that Debtor could be said to have acquired rights in the collateral is July 1 (since under Article 2, Debtor acquired rights only as the machine's component parts were designated by the manufacturer as ones which he would use; §2-501(1)(b)). Under B.C. §547(c)(3), Bank has not received its security interest on account of antecedent debt, since perfection occurred within ten days of attachment. Without the protection of this section, Bank's interest might be attacked as a preference, since more than ten days elapsed between the giving of value and the perfection. See Coogan, §9C.06[6][d][iii].

d. Net result rule: The final modification of the antecedency concept occurs in §547(c)(4). This section adopts the so-called *"net result"* rule. This rule in effect gives the secured party who takes security for antecedent debt credit for any later advances.

Example: Secured party is owed $10,000 by Debtor. On February 1, Debtor gives Secured Party $2,500 of security against this antecedent debt. On March 1, Secured Party makes a $2,500 unsecured loan. If §547(c)(4) did not exist, the security interest would be wiped out as having been made on account of antecedent debt, and Secured Party would not have received credit for the subsequent $2,500 advance. With the application of (c)(4), the later advance of $2,500 resuscitates the $2,500 of security interest, which cannot be attacked as a preference. See Coogan, §9C.06[6][d][iv].

4. Presumption of insolvency: Requirement five is that the transfer have been made while the debtor was *insolvent*. Two points are important. First, as set forth below, the transfer is deemed "made", usually, only when it was perfected; if the secured party delays perfecting until shortly before bankruptcy, the insolvency requirement will be met even though the original loan may have been made, and the security agreement signed, while the debtor was perfectly solvent. Secondly, §547(f) creates a *presumption* that the debtor was insolvent throughout the 90 days prior to filing of the petition. (Also, a requirement in the old Act, that at the time of the transfer, the transferee had "reason to believe" that the debtor was insolvent, has been dropped from the new Code.)

   a. Insider provision: But where the transferee is an insider, and the transfer took place more than 90 days but less than a year prior to the filing of the petition, there is *no presumption* of insolvency, and the trustee must bear the burden of proving insolvency at the time of the transfer.

5. Less than ninety days before petition: The sixth requirement is that the transfer have occurred *less than 90 days prior to bankruptcy*. This represents a shortening from the old Act, where the transfer merely had to be made within four months prior to bankruptcy. Observe that it is the *transfer* that must occur within 90 days, not the underlying debt. Thus the secured party who makes a loan long before bankruptcy, but delays perfecting until the eve of bankruptcy, will fall within the 90-day period, since the transfer is deemed made only when perfected (*infra*, pp. 140-41).

   a. One year for insiders: If the transferee is an *"insider"* with respect to the debtor, then the transfer may be attacked even if it occurred as long as *one year* prior to the bankruptcy. "Insider" is defined in §101(25) to include various types of individuals or entities who have a sufficiently close relationship with the debtor that the transaction should be subjected to close scrutiny. If the debtor is a person, his relatives, and corporations or partnerships which he controls, are insiders. If the debtor is a corporation, its directors, officers, controlling stockholders, and each of their relatives, are insiders.

6. Greater share than in liquidation: The final element of a preference is that the transfer must enable the creditor to receive *more than he would have received if*: (1) the transfer had not been made; and (2) the creditor had received merely his pro rata share as part of a Chapter 7 (straight bankruptcy) liquidation.

   a. Payments to secured creditor: This requirement has one extremely important result for the secured creditor: to the extent that a secured party has a valid security interest, *cash payments* made to him are *not preferences*, even though they come within 90 days of the bankruptcy petition.

     Example: Secured Party has a valid, promptly perfected, security interest in Debtor's property on January 1; the debt is $10,000, and the collateral is worth $8,000. On June 1,

Debtor makes cash payments to Secured Party of $8,000, on account of the previous debt. On July 1, Debtor files a bankruptcy petition. Because the trustee would not be able to attack the security interest itself as a preference (or for any other reason), Secured Party would have been entitled to the $8,000 in a Chapter 7 straight liquidation, had he not received the June 1 payment. Therefore, he has not received more than he would have in straight bankruptcy, and the seventh requirement for a preferential transfer is not met. The trustee cannot recover the payment.

b. **Time of transfer:** It seems likely that in evaluating what the creditor would have gotten in a strict bankruptcy liquidation, one should assume that the liquidation occurs *at the time of the transfer*. See W&S, p. 1005. Thus in the above example, even if Debtor somehow squandered Secured Party's collateral between June 1 and the July 1 bankruptcy petition, the "greater share than in bankruptcy" requirement is not satisfied, because the requirement is evaluated as of June 1 (time of the cash transfer), not July 1 (filing of the petition).

E. **When grant of security interest deemed "made":** Recall that one of the two policies implemented by the preferential transfers provision is to *discourage secret liens*. The way §547 does this is to fix the time that a "transfer" is deemed made as the *date the security interest was perfected, not the date on which it was created*. (An exception, where perfection occurs within ten days of creation, is discussed below.)

1. **How this is done:** This result is produced by B.C. §547(e)(2), which provides that a transfer is deemed "made . . . (B) at the time such transfer is perfected, if such transfer is perfected after . . . ten days [following creation of the security interest]. . . ." Perfection is defined under §547(e)(1)(B) as the time after which "a creditor on a simple contract cannot acquire a judicial lien that is superior to the interest of the [secured party]." Since under UCC §9-301(1)(b) a lien creditor has priority over an unperfected security interest, perfection within the UCC's definition is always the equivalent of perfection as the term is defined in B.C. §547(e)(1)(B).

2. **Significance:** The practical effect of this definition of the time of transfer is that even if the secured party advances full value in return for his security interest, and even though the interest and the loan are both created long before the 90-day period, there will be a preference if *perfection* does not occur until inside the 90-day period.

   Example: Bank lends Debtor $10,000 in June, 1978. At that time, a security interest in Debtor's receivables and inventory is given to Bank. Bank neglects to file a financing statement.

On September 1, 1980, Bank finally files (perhaps because it has heard that Debtor is now in precarious financial condition). On October 1, Debtor files for bankruptcy. Since perfection occurred on September 1, 1980, that is the time the transfer was deemed "made". This means that the transfer is: (1) for or on account of antecedent debt, since the debt was contracted two years previously; (2) the transfer was made while Debtor was insolvent (even though he may not have been insolvent in June of 1978); and (3) the transfer occurs within 90 days prior to the bankruptcy petition (even though the security interest itself existed, as between the debtor and the secured party, long before that.) If the transfer were deemed made at the time the security interest was **created**, neither §547 nor anything else in the Bankruptcy Code would enable the trustee to knock down Bank's interest, and it would be rewarded for having kept its security interest secret (perhaps misleading other creditors who subsequently extended credit in reliance on the record.)

3. **Ten-day grace period:** An important exception to the "transfer made when interest perfected" rule is that if the security interest is *perfected within ten days of when it was created*, the transfer is deemed made *at the time the interest was created*. Thus so long as the secured party perfects within ten days of the time at which he advances value and obtains his security interest, there can be no preference. (This is true even if the whole transaction takes place within the 90-day period.)

> **Example:** Debtor is in horrendous financial condition, and is in fact insolvent. He persuades Finance Co. to make him a loan on February 1, in return for a security interest in his last unencumbered asset, his automobile. A security agreement is signed that same day, Feb. 1, and Finance Co. perfects on Feb. 8. Debtor files a bankruptcy petition on Feb. 15. Finance Co.'s security interest is not a preference. Since it was perfected with ten days of creation, the transfer of the interest is deemed made when it was created, Feb. 1. Since the loan was made that same day, there was no transfer "for or on account of antecedent debt." Therefore, even though the whole transaction took place within the 90 days prior to bankruptcy, no preference resulted.

VII. THE "FLOATING LIEN" AND THE PREFERENTIAL TRANSFER RULE

A. **Definition of "floating lien":** UCC §9-204(1) validates what is popularly called the *"floating lien"*, a type of security interest in *after-acquired property*. The operation of the floating lien is demonstrated by the following example, which will serve as a scenario for much of our later discussion of B.C. §547(c)(5) and the floating lien.

> **Example:** Dealer, who wishes to expand his retail appliance business, seeks long-term financing from Bank. Dealer wishes to have a $100,000 "line of credit" — that is, he wishes to be able to borrow, at any time, such that his total indebtedness is no more than $100,000. With this line of credit, he will be able to buy appliances from manufacturers as he increases his business; he will also be able to extend credit, in turn, to his customers, who buy on retail installment contracts.
>
> Bank and Dealer therefore execute a security agreement which covers "inventory and accounts receivable." Furthermore, and most importantly, the security agreement covers ***after-acquired property*** and ***future advances***. Thus, any collateral that Dealer later acquires, such as a new shipment of appliances, is covered by the security agreement; similarly, any time in the future that Bank advances new money, this money is secured by the security interest in all of Dealer's inventory and accounts receivable.
>
> Since the particular items of inventory and accounts are constantly changing (as inventory is acquired and sold, and as accounts are created and then destroyed by payment), Bank's security interest is said to "float" over this ever-changing unspecified mass of collateral.
>
> This security agreement is executed on January 1, and a financing statement is promptly filed. On the same day, Bank makes its first advance to Dealer of $10,000. The security interest is thus perfected (UCC§9-303(1)). Bank makes new advances in the next few months, and Dealer buys new inventory and acquires new accounts as the inventory is sold. On March 1, Dealer has borrowed the whole $100,000 from Bank, and Dealer's inventory and accounts on that date total $80,000 (all of which is covered by Bank's security interest).
>
> During the next 90 days, Bank refuses to lend any more money, nor does Dealer make any loan repayment. The value of Bank's collateral during this 90-day period drops from $80,000 on March 1 to a low of $60,000 on April 15. At that point, Bank attempts to force Debtor to build the collateral back up by saying that it will foreclose unless Dealer spends all of his money on new inventory and none to pay off other creditors. The value of the collateral climbs to $100,000 (the amount of the loan), where it stands on June 1, on which date Dealer files a bankruptcy petition.

1. **Trustee's lines of attack:** If the general provisions of B.C. §547 applied, the trustee of Dealer, in the above example, could make at least two reasonably potent arguments about why all or at least some of the $100,000 worth of accounts and inventory (as of the date of bankruptcy) represent a preference to Bank:

    a. **No rights in collateral at time of filing:** First, the trustee can make the following broad-based syllogism: (1) the transfer of a security interest is deemed "made" under§547(e)(1)(B) and (2) when it is so far perfected that a lien creditor could no longer have priority over it. (*Supra*, p. 140.) (2) Under UCC §9-203(1)(c) and §9-303(1), a security interest cannot be perfected against a lien creditor until the ***debtor has rights in the collateral***. (3) What Bank is claiming is a security interest in accounts many of which did not come into existence except within 90 days prior to bankruptcy, and in inventory that was not acquired by Dealer until less than 90 days before bankruptcy. Therefore, as to each new account and each new item of inventory, the transfer occurred within the 90-day period, and was made on account of antecedent debt. Under this argument, if it prevails, the trustee will be able to avoid Bank's security interest in all or most of the accounts and inventory (every account and inventory item in which the debtor did not have rights on March 1.)

    b. **Improvement of position:** Even if this argument fails, the trustee can argue somewhat persuasively that by forcing Dealer to build the collateral back up during the 90-day period, Bank has improved its position at the expense of general creditors; this is exactly the sort of unequal treatment (indeed collusion) that the preferential transfer rule is designed to prevent. If this argument is accepted, the trustee will at least be able to avoid the last $20,000 of accounts and inventory (the amount by which Bank improved its position during the 90-day period.)

2. **Two cases reject trustee's argument:** But two federal Court of Appeals cases, both decided in 1969 under the old Bankruptcy Act, rejected the first of these arguments explicitly, and the second at least implicitly.

    a. ***Grain Merchants:*** In *Grain Merchants of Indiana, Inc. v. Union Bank and Savings Co.*, 408 F.2d 209 (7th Cir. 1969), the Seventh Circuit rejected an argument like that in Paragraph (a), *supra*, by three different lines of reasoning: (1) at the time the secured party filed its floating lien, it became absolutely protected against having a subsequent lien creditor take priority over its interest, so that it was at this moment of filing that the transfer is deemed "made". (2) The secured party's security interest was in the "entity of the accounts receivable as a whole" and not in the individual components, so that the transfer occurred at the time the security interest in the "mass" of accounts receivable was created and filed. (3) On the particular facts of *Grain Merchants*, as new accounts receivable were created during the period shortly before bankruptcy, the secured party allowed the debtor to keep the cash collected from older accounts; thus there was "substitution of collateral".

   i. No improvement of position: The court in *Grain Merchants* did stress, in connection with its third line of reasoning, that the secured party did not improve its position during the period just before bankruptcy (four months, rather than ninety days, under the old Bankruptcy Act.) But even if there had been an improvement in position, it is hard to see how this would have been objectionable under the court's first and second arguments.

   b. *DuBay v. Williams*: Similarly, in *DuBay v. Williams*, 417 F.2d 1277 (9th Cir. 1969), the Ninth Circuit held that the transfer of the security interest occurred at the time the secured party filed, since no lien creditor could thereafter take priority. Since this filing occurred long before the four-month period, the entire transaction was immune. Also, the court noted that the secured party's floating lien was easily ascertainable by any creditor who looked at the record, and that therefore no creditor could have been misled into believing that the debtor's receivables would constitute assets available to pay other debts.

B. Improvement of position: The possibility that a secured party might cause the debtor to build up the collateral during the 90 day period, at the expense of other creditors troubled the persons who drafted the new Bankruptcy Code. Therefore, they adopted a "middle" position on the floating lien, which in essence neither strikes down nor completely validates after-acquired inventory and receivables clauses. Under B.C. §547(5), the secured party's interest is upheld *only to the extent that he did not improve his position during the 90-day period* prior to bankruptcy. (Thus §547(c)(5) invalidates some of the reasoning, though probably not the result, in *Grain Merchants* and *DuBay*.)

   1. Text of §547(c)(5): B.C. §547(c)(5) states that the trustee may not invalidate as a preference "a perfected security interest in *inventory* or a *receivable* or the proceeds of either, except to the extent that the aggregate of all such transfers to the transferee caused a *reduction*, as of the date of the filing of the petition and to the *prejudice of other creditors* holding unsecured claims, of any amount by which the debt secured by such security interest exceeded the value of all security interest for such debt . . . 90 days before the date of the filing of the petition. . . ." (emphasis added). (The evaluation date is 90 days before the filing of the petition unless the transaction involved an insider, or the first advance under the security agreement was made less than 90 days before the filing of the petition; as to these exceptions, see *infra*, p. 147.)

2. **How §547(c)(5) works:** Thus in the normal case where the secured party is not an insider, and the loan or other value is given more than 90 days before bankruptcy, the value of the collateral and the amount of the debt must be measured as of two dates: (1) 90 days before the petition is filed; and (2) the day the petition is filed. Based on the results for these days, the following rules apply:

  a. **Fully secured 90 days before:** If the secured party is *fully secured* 90 days before bankruptcy, *there can be no preference*. This is true even if at some point during the 90 days the value of the collateral drops so that the secured party is not fully secured, and then climbs back up.

    Example: 90 days before bankruptcy, Secured Party is owed $10,000, and he has a security interest in inventory which at that moment has a value of $11,000. 45 days before bankruptcy, the value of the inventory drops to $5,000. By the date of bankruptcy, it has climbed back to $11,000. There has been no preferential transfer; the only relevant dates are 90 days before filing and the day of filing, and the fact that Secured Party was not fully secured at some point in between is irrelevant.

  b. **Position not improved:** Even if the collateral is worth less than the debt 90 days before bankruptcy, if this gap (the amount of unsecured indebtedness) *does not increase* during the 90-day period, there is no preference. (However, any payments made to the secured party must be added back to the value of the debt on the date of bankruptcy before measuring this gap.)

    Example: 90 days before bankruptcy, Secured Party is owed $10,000, and holds a security interest in Debtor's inventory which has a present value of $5,000. No payments to Secured Party are made during the 90-day period. On the date of bankruptcy, the inventory is still worth $5,000. Even though the particular items of inventory may have changed during the 90-day period, there is no preference. Similarly, if $1,000 had been paid to Secured Party during the 90-day period, and the value of the collateral had decreased from $5,000 to $4,000, there would have been no preference. But if $1,000 had been paid to Secured Party, and the value of the collateral had remained the same, there would be a preference of $1,000, assuming that the other requirements for a preference (e.g., that the payment was made to the prejudice of unsecured creditors) are satisfied.

c. **Must be "transfer":** Even if the gap between the value of the collateral and the value of the debt does increase during the 90-day period, there is no preference unless the increase in the gap is the result of one or more "transfers" to the secured party.

Example: 90 days before Brewer's bankruptcy, Bank is owed $10,000, and holds a security interest in Brewer's inventory, which inventory is worth $5,000. During the 90-day period, the value of this inventory increases not because the physical volume of inventory increases, but rather, because of natural aging, or fluctuations in market value. On the date of bankruptcy, Bank is still owed $10,000, but the collateral is now worth $9,000. Even though the unsecured gap has decreased, this is not the result of any "transfer" to Secured Party, since the same physical mass of collateral remains. Therefore, there is no preference.

d. **"To the prejudice of unsecured creditors":** Finally, even if there is a diminution in the gap between value of the collateral and amount of the debt during the 90 days, and even if this diminution results from "transfers" to the secured party, there will be no preference if these transfers are not *prejudicial to other, unsecured, creditors*.

Example: 90 days before Carpenter's bankruptcy, he owes $10,000 to Bank. Bank has an interest in Carpenter's inventory, which has a value of $5,000 at that time. During the 90 days before bankruptcy, Carpenter works on his existing stock of raw wood, and converts it to much more valuable finished furniture; he does not buy any new lumber. At the day of filing of the bankruptcy petition, the collateral is now worth $11,000. Even though the creation of furniture out of raw wood might be considered to be a "transfer" for the benefit of Bank, this transfer is not prejudicial to other, unsecured, creditors. That is, the transfer has not been accomplished by Carpenter's failure to pay his general creditors, Therefore, there is no preference. If, by contrast, the value of the inventory had been increased by Carpenter's acquisition of additional lumber or finished pieces from suppliers who sold on unsecured credit, the decrease in the gap would be to the prejudice of unsecured creditors (namely, those who supplied the raw finished materials). Then, the decrease in the gap would constitute a preference.

   i. Ambiguous cases: Of course, it may sometimes be difficult to decide whether a given build-up of the collateral is prejudicial to unsecured creditors. For instance, suppose that in the above example, Carpenter had a number of workers working for him, and the only way he was able to pay these workers during the 90 days before bankruptcy was to fail to pay his unsecured creditors (e.g., his landlord.) If the value of Carpenter's inventory were increased because of the work done by these employees, would this increase in value be at the expense of general creditors? White and Summers suggest that in this type of case, "the causal connection between the accretion in value of the collateral and the failure to pay other creditors once removed is too tenuous;" therefore, they suggest that the requisite prejudice to other creditors should be found lacking, or that no transfer be found to have occurred. W&S, p. 1011.

3. **Measuring value:** When the court determines whether the secured creditor's position improved during the 90 days before the filing of the petition, it must of course measure the "value" of the collateral at the beginning and end of this 90-day period. How should this value be measured? The choice is usually between the collateral's value as part of an *ongoing business* and its value in a *liquidation sale*. There is no fixed rule about which of these measures should be used. Courts tend to use "ongoing concern" value in Chapter 9, 11, and 13 cases (where the business is being continued) and "liquidation" value in Chapter 7 cases (where the business itself is being liquidated), but this is merely a rule of thumb, and is sometimes disregarded. See, e.g., *In re Lackow Brothers, Inc.*, 752 F.2d 1529 (11th Cir. 1985) (In Chapter 7 case, trial court correctly used the "ongoing concern" rather than "liquidation" value because this was the value shown in the debtor's own accounting records, and was the only reliable evidence of what the collateral was worth 90 days before the filing; the fact that the eventual forced sale indicated a much lower value for the collateral was irrelevant.)

4. **Insiders and transactions shortly before bankruptcy:** There are two exceptions to the general rule that the unsecured "gap" on the filing date is compared with the gap 90 days before bankruptcy.

   a. Insiders: First, if the secured party is an *"insider"* (see *supra*, p. 139), the value of the collateral and the amount of the debt as of *one year before bankruptcy* is used, rather than the value and debt 90 days before bankruptcy. (This corresponds to the general one-year preference period for insider transactions.)

b. **First value less than 90 days before petition:** Secondly, if the *first value* is given by the secured party *less than 90 days* prior to bankruptcy, the date on which that first value is given applies.

> **Example:** On February 1, Bank lends $10,000 to Debtor, and takes a security interest in his receivables, which at that point have a value of $8,000. On March 1, Debtor files a bankruptcy petition; on that date, the accounts are still worth $8,000. Since the first value under the security agreement was given less than 90 days before bankruptcy, the gap is evaluated as of that day. Since this gap has not increased by the date of bankruptcy, there is no preference. This is so even though the value of Debtor's accounts may have been only $4,000 on December 1 of the previous year (90 days before bankruptcy.)

5. **Applies only to accounts and inventory:** The special rule of B.C. §547(c)(5) applies only to after-acquired property interests in *accounts receivable* and *inventory*. Thus it does not apply, for instance, to after-acquired clauses covering *equipment*.

> **Example:** Bank lends $10,000 to Debtor, taking a security interest in all equipment which Debtor presently owns or thereafter acquires (which equipment then has a value of $8,000). Less than 90 days prior to bankruptcy, Debtor acquires a new machine which he will use in his business, which has a value of $2,000. Debtor pays for the machine by selling a different machine, and using the $2,000 cash proceeds to buy the new machine. Since the machine is neither inventory nor proceeds, it is not saved from being a preference by §547(c)(5). Therefore, it is probably a preference under §547(b), even though Bank's position did not improve during the 90-day period (since it lost its collateral in the other machine, which had the same value as the new one.) See W&S, p. 1010.

6. **Effect on *Grain Merchants* and *DuBay* cases:** Suppose that a secured party is unable to bring himself within the terms of a §547(c)(5)'s saving clause (i.e., he improved his position during the 90-day period at the expense of unsecured creditors.) May he nonetheless argue that under the holding in *DuBay* (*supra*, p. 144) and the alternate holding in *Grain Merchants* (*supra*, p. 143), there is no preference because his "floating lien" was perfected at the time of filing, which occurred more than 90 days before bankruptcy? This argument is explicitly foreclosed by §547(e)(3), which provides that for purposes of defining the time at which a transfer is made, "a transfer is not made until the debtor has *acquired rights* in the

property transferred" (emphasis added). Thus when a new account arises, or a new inventory item is acquired, the transfer of the security interest in that account or inventory item is only then made. Filing by itself can no longer constitute a "transfer" of accounts which do not yet exist or inventory items which have not yet been acquired.

7. **Perfection required:** §547(c)(5)'s saving clause also applies only to a "*perfected* security interest in inventory or a receivable. . . ." (Emphasis added.) Presumably, this means that the security interest must be perfected as of ninety days before bankruptcy (or one year before in the case of an outsider, and on the date value is given, in the case of an arrangement commencing less than 90 days before bankruptcy.) Thus if the floating lienor has not filed his financing statement 90 days before bankruptcy, his entire interest will be struck down as a preference even if he does not improve his relative position during the 90 days.

VIII. PROCEEDS IN BANKRUPTCY

A. **Proceeds outside of bankruptcy:** We have seen above (*supra*, pp. 92-98) operation of the Code with respect to proceeds in a non-bankruptcy context.

B. **Proceeds in insolvency under §9-306(4):** If the debtor goes bankrupt (or otherwise becomes insolvent, as where he goes into receivership under state law) UCC §9-306(4) purports to set forth the extent of the secured party's interest in proceeds.

1. **Not entitled to all identifiable proceeds:** Whereas before insolvency, the secured party has an interest in *all* identifiable proceeds, such is not the case after insolvency under §9-306(4). Instead, §9-306(4) provides that the secured party who has a perfected proceeds security interest has a perfected interest in:

   a. identifiable *non-cash* proceeds;

   b. *bank accounts* which contain *only* proceeds;

   c. identifiable *cash proceeds* in the form of *money* which is *not commingled* with other money and *not deposited in a bank account* prior to insolvency;

   d. identifiable *cash proceeds* in the form of *checks* and the like which are *not deposited in a bank account* prior to insolvency; and

   e. *all cash and bank accounts* of the debtor, if other cash proceeds have been commingled or deposited in a bank account; however, the cash or bank account interest is *limited* to "an amount *not greater than the amount of any cash proceeds*

received by the debtor within ten days before the institu-
tion of the insolvency proceedings less the sum of (I) the
payments to the secured party on account of cash proceeds
received by the debtor during such period and (II) the cash
proceeds received by the debtor during such period to which
the secured party is entitled under [Pars. (a)-(c) above.]" UCC
§9-306(4)(d)(ii).

2. **Meaning of "identifiable":** While the Code does not define the
term "identifiable," there is usually little difficulty in identifying
non-cash proceeds ((a) above). An example of such proceeds is a
trade-in car received by a car dealer. Similarly, there is not much
difficulty in "identifying" the money cash proceeds ((c) above), and
the check cash proceeds ((d) above), since by definition the cash
proceeds in (c) and (d) have not been commingled or deposited in a
bank account. In other words, they have been segregated, and the
secured creditor can point to them as the particular cash received
when the debtor disposed of the collateral.

3. **No identifiability requirement for bank accounts:** With
respect to cash which has been commingled or deposited in a bank
account, there is no requirement of identifiability imposed by §9-
306(4)(d). This represents a substantial change from pre-UCC law,
by which "the secured party, if he could identify the proceeds, could
reclaim them or their equivalent from the debtor or his trustee in
bankruptcy." (Emphasis added.) (Comment 2, §9-306). Thus a
secured party is no longer required to show in bankruptcy that the
particular funds present in the debtor's bank account at bankruptcy
are indeed the same dollars the debtor received by disposing of the
collateral. The need for complicated tracing arguments (e.g., LIFO,
"lowest intermediate balance," etc.) is therefore eliminated in bankruptcy.

   a. **Tracing still required outside of insolvency:** Note, how-
     ever, that §9-306(4)(d) applies only in *insolvency*. In other
     situations, the secured party has an interest solely in *identifi-*
     able proceeds (§9-306(2)), and where the proceeds have been
     deposited in a bank account containing deposits from other
     sources, the secured party will still have to "trace" his
     proceeds.

4. **Operation of §9-306(4)(d):** Although there is some dispute about
exactly how §9-306(4)(d) is to be interpreted, the following steps
seem to be the correct ones. (See 2 Gilmore 1338, written before
the 1972 re-write to §9-306(4)(d), but still basically accurate).

   a. Determine the amount of cash proceeds (*from disposition of*
     the secured party's collateral) that the debtor received dur-
     ing the ten days before bankruptcy which the debtor either: (i)

deposited in an account containing funds from other sources; or (ii) commingled with cash from other sources.

b. Subtract the amount of any proceeds that the debtor has paid over to the secured party on account of proceeds received by the debtor during this ten-day period; and

c. Subtract any sums to which the secured party is entitled under Par. 1(a), (b), (c), and (d) above (p. 149) (e.g., uncommingled cash or undeposited checks, remaining in the debtor's possession on the date of bankruptcy.)

> **Example:** Ten days before Debtor goes bankrupt, Finance Co. is owed $20,000 by him. This debt is secured by a security interest in Debtor's inventory (and in the proceeds of that inventory.) During the ten days before bankruptcy, Debtor collects $10,000 on account of sales of inventory (some of which sales actually accrued prior to the ten-day period.) Also during the ten days, Debtor receives $5,000 in the form of payment of a long-overdue account. This account was not collateral as to Finance Co. (since the account existed before Finance Co.'s security inventory ever existed); however, it was collateral as to Factor, who had a security interest in all of Debtor's accounts receivable. This $5,000 is deposited in Debtor's general bank account. Of the $10,000 collected from inventory sales, $7,000 is deposited in the same general bank account. $1,000 is paid to Finance Co. Also, Debtor takes another $2,000 from his general bank account and pays it to Finance Co.; this represents money from inventory sold by Debtor more than ten days before bankruptcy (which Debtor should have paid over to Finance Co. earlier but did not.) The remaining $2,000 of the $10,000 collected from inventory during the ten-day period is held on the date of bankruptcy in the form of cash and a special inventory-proceeds-only bank account. The general account has $9,000 in it on the date of bankruptcy.
>
> Finance Co. is of course entitled to the $2,000 in cash and special-account proceeds on hand on the bankruptcy date. In determining the amount of money from the *general* account to which Finance Co. is entitled, the following calculations must be made: (1) The total proceeds from inventory collected by Finance Co. in the ten days before bankruptcy is $10,000. (2) Subtract the $1,000 of this money actually paid to Finance Co. (3) Subtract the $2,000 of this money actually on hand (to which Finance Co. is entitled). This leaves $7,000 from the general bank account, to which Finance Co. is entitled.

Observe that this solution ignores two sums: (1) the $2,000 paid to Finance Co. is not penalized; and (2) the $5,000 collected on account of **other parties'** collateral, which even though it is deposited to the bank account does not benefit Finance Co. To view the matter another way, Finance Co. is entitled to receive from the general (commingled) bank account a sum sufficient to give it the same total amount of proceeds as it would have received had Debtor paid over to it immediately all sums Debtor received from the disposition of Finance Co.'s collateral during the ten days prior to bankruptcy.

5. ***In re Gibson Products:*** Observe that in our listing of steps to be followed, and in our example, we have assumed that in the phrase "the amount of any cash proceeds received by the debtor within ten days before [insolvency]" (§9-306(4)(d)(ii)), "cash proceeds" refers solely to proceeds from the disposition of the ***particular secured party's collateral***. However, at least one court has taken a contrary view. This was the case of *In re Gibson Products of Arizona*, 543 F.2d 652 (9th Cir. 1976).

   a. **Facts of *Gibson Products*:** In *Gibson Products*, Arizona Wholesale sold the debtor certain types of appliances, which were inventory to the debtor. Arizona had a validly perfected security interest in the inventory and in its proceeds. During the ten days before bankruptcy, the debtor deposited over $19,000 in cash into its bank account. However, Arizona was only able to show that $10 of it represented sales of inventory covered by Arizona's security interest. (It is not clear what the source was for the rest of the $19,000.) Since Arizona was owed over $28,000, it made claim for the entire $19,000 deposited to the account (which was the debtor's general, commingled, bank account.)

   b. **Holding:** The Ninth Circuit rejected the view that under §9-306(4)(d)(ii), only deposits from the proceeds of sale of the particular secured party's collateral may be awarded to that secured party. Thus the fact that Arizona showed that only $10 of the deposit represented proceeds from the sale of Arizona's collateral, did not prevent Arizona from being entitled, under §9-306(4), to the entire sum deposited in the ten-day period.

   c. **Found to be preference:** However, the court went on to find, as a matter of federal law, that to the extent that the $19,000 exceeded the proceeds received during the ten-day period from the sale of Arizona's own collateral, this excess was a ***preference*** voidable by the trustee in bankruptcy.

   d. Criticism: This approach seems clearly wrong. As White and Summers (p. 1016) put it, 9-306(4)(d)(ii) "means that the secured creditor gets no more from a bank account than the amount of proceeds from *his* collateral that he can prove that the debtor received within the ten days prior to the filing of the petition. . . .The Ninth Circuit view that 'any cash proceeds' as to one creditor includes the proceeds of another's collateral is not defensible. Why should one creditor have a greater claim in proceeds of a second creditor than he has in any other cash that might come through the cash register as the result of the services or the sale of other goods?" However, White and Summers conclude that the *outcome* in *Gibson Products* is correct; if only $10 was received as the proceeds of Arizona's collateral during the ten-day period, this is the limit on its recovery; but this result should be reached as a matter of interpretation of 9-306, not as a matter of federal bankruptcy preference law. (W&S, p. 1016).

6. Proceeds interest as preference: §9-306(4)(d) on its face appears to apply only to the problem of determining what the rights of a secured creditor are to a debtor's commingled bank account. Yet at least one court has used the section for a broader purpose, that of determining whether a *preference* under the federal bankruptcy law existed.

   a. *Fitzpatrick v. Philco:* In *Fitzpatrick v. Philco Finance Corp.*, 491 F.2d 1288 (7th Cir. 1974), during the week before bankruptcy, the debtor paid to its secured creditor (Philco) over $44,000. Yet, the debtor received and deposited only $4,500 of proceeds from the sale of covered collateral during the ten days prior to bankruptcy.

   b. All cash proceeds asserted covered: Philco argued that §9-306(4)(d)(ii)'s limitation to the amount of "any cash proceeds" received by the debtor within ten days referred to all receipts from *whatever source* deposited in the bank account, rather than merely to receipts from the sale of Philco's collateral. (This was the argument that later prevailed in *Gibson Products, supra* p. 152.) But the Seventh Circuit flatly rejected this argument, holding that " 'any cash proceeds' . . . must mean *cash proceeds from the sale of collateral in which the creditor had a security interest.*" (Emphasis added).

   c. Preference found: The Seventh Circuit then found that to the extent that the payments to Philco ($44,000) during the ten days prior to bankruptcy exceeded the amount received from disposition of Philco's collateral ($4,500), Philco had received a *preference* which must be returned to the trustee.

d. Continued validity in doubt: The payments to Philco do seem to have some of the attributes of a preference, since Philco did apparently improve its position dramatically during the last ten days prior to bankruptcy. However, the precise holding in *Fitzpatrick* (that there is a preference as to any payments to the secured party during the ten-day period in excess of proceeds of covered collateral that are deposited in the debtor's bank account) is probably ***no longer valid*** in light of the new Bankruptcy Code.

i. §9-306(4)(d) irrelevant: First, UCC §9-306(4)(d) does not seem to be the appropriate vehicle for determining whether a preference exists. The *Fitzpatrick* court was willing to let Philco keep the $4,500, because this was the sum that had been deposited in the debtor's bank account in the ten-day period. Yet suppose that the debtor had simply kept the $4,500 in cash on hand, and that this cash was still in his possession on the date of bankruptcy. Under the *Fitzpatrick* court's rationale, Philco would no longer be entitled to even the $4,500, because this sum never passed through the debtor's bank account It does not seem sensible to make the existence and size of a preference turn on what passes through the debtor's bank account during the ten-day period. See W&S, p. 1015. White and Summers argue that to the extent that §9-306 is relevant at all, the issue should be what proceeds from the sale of collateral the debtor has ***received*** in the ten-day period (regardless of whether these proceeds have been deposited in his bank account). (*Id.*)

ii. Improvement of position: Secondly, although the new Bankruptcy Code does not deal with the particular problems of proceeds as preferences, the spirit of B.C. §547(c)(5) is that (at least as to inventory and receivables and the proceeds of each), only two dates are relevant: 90 days before the filing of the petition, and the date of bankruptcy. It is only if the secured party improves his position from the first of these days to the second that he has received a preference. This conflicts quite sharply with the rationale of *Fitzpatrick*.

Example: Suppose, for instance, that 90 days before the debtor's bankruptcy in *Fitzpatrick*, Philco was fully secured. Under B.C. 547(c)(5), nothing that Philco could have received from the debtor during the ten days before bankruptcy (or at any time during the 90-day period) could have given rise to a preference, assuming that the proceeds paid over were from inventory or receivables. Yet under the *Fitzpatrick* rationale, so long as payments made by the debtor to Philco within ten days before bankruptcy exceeded proceeds received by the debtor during this period, there would be a preference to the extent of the excess.

This approach penalizes a creditor in Philco's position for the unhappy accident of having received part of its money during the ten-day period, a penalty that is nowhere suggested by the Bankruptcy Code. Instead, the problem should be solved solely by a determination of whether Philco improved its position during the 90 days before bankruptcy. (The amount to which Philco might be entitled in the debtor's general bank account might, when added to other payments made to Philco, constitute an improvement in Philco's position, in which case there would be a preference. But the money in the bank account would not have a different status from any sums transferred during the 90-day period.)

7. **Statutory lien attack on UCC §9-306(4):** There is an outside chance that a trustee in bankruptcy could successfully challenge the entire principle of UCC §9-306(4) (that an interest in various sorts of proceeds becomes fixed and enforceable upon insolvency.) Under B.C. §545, the trustee is entitled to avoid certain "*statutory liens*", including any lien which "first becomes effective against the debtor (A) when a case under this title concerning the debtor is commenced. . . ." A trustee might argue that §9-306(4), since it applies only upon insolvency, is precisely the sort of statutory lien that B.C. §545 avoids. However, since §9-306(4) actually *cuts back* on a secured party's rights, compared with what they were under pre-Code "tracing" rules, the courts will probably not accept this argument. See W&S, p. 1017.

IX. SELLER'S RIGHT OF RECLAMATION IN BANKRUPTCY

A. **Reclamation in general:** Suppose a hopelessly insolvent person purchases goods from a seller, by *misrepresenting* his *financial condition*. No security agreement is executed, and the sale is made on open credit. If the buyer goes bankrupt without paying for the goods, is there any way the seller can avoid being treated as a general (unsecured) creditor in bankruptcy?

1. **UCC right to reclaim:** UCC §2-702(2) does provide some relief to the seller in this situation. That section states that "Where the seller discovers that the buyer has received goods on credit while insolvent he may reclaim the goods upon demand made within ten days after the receipt, but if misrepresentation of solvency has been made to the particular seller in writing within three months before delivery the ten day limitation does not apply." In other words, if the buyer was insolvent when he got the goods, the seller can

reclaim them within the next ten days whether or not the buyer misrepresented his insolvency. Any time after the ten-day period, the seller may reclaim if the buyer had made a ***written misrepresentation*** of his solvency in the three months before the goods were delivered.

2. **Status in bankruptcy:** However, a seller's rights under §2-702(2) do not entirely survive if the buyer goes bankrupt. B.C. §546(c) preserves any common-law right of a seller to reclaim, but lists two limitations: (1) "such a seller may not reclaim any such goods unless such seller demands ***in writing*** reclamation of such goods before ***ten days after receipt*** of such goods by the debtor" (emphasis added) and (2) "the court may deny reclamation to a seller with such a right of reclamation that has made such a demand . . . if [the] court (A) grants the claim of such a seller priority as an administrative expense; or (B) secures such claim by a lien."

   a. **How this cuts back UCC right:** Thus the UCC right of reclamation is cut back in two significant respects. First of all, the right is completely cut off once ten days from delivery of the goods have elapsed, and the seller has not made a written demand for reclamation. In other words, the UCC right to reclaim within three months if there has been a written misrepresentation of solvency is ***not honored in the bankruptcy context***. Secondly, the court may choose, rather than giving the seller back his goods, to give the seller merely "priority as an administrative expense"; if the debtor's estate is so small that it cannot even cover administrative expenses (e.g., the cost of the trustee), the seller may not receive anything.

3. **Conflict with holder of security in after-acquired items:** UCC §2-702(3) provides that the seller's right of reclamation is "subject to the rights of a buyer in ordinary course or other good faith purchaser. . . ." It is quite clear that if the buyer immediately resells the goods to a purchaser in good faith, the seller cannot reclaim them. But what happens if the buyer has a creditor who holds a security interest in the buyer's ***after acquired property***; is such a creditor a "good-faith purchaser" who prevails over the reclaiming seller? At least one court has held that such a secured party is indeed a "purchaser" under the broad definition of "purchase" in UCC §1-201(32), and that the secured party, not the seller, gets the goods. *In re Samuels & Co., Inc.*, 526 F.2d 1238 (5th Cir. 1976).

DEFAULT

Introductory Note: This chapter will examine what happens when the debtor falls behind in his payments, or commits some other event of "default" under the security agreement. Normally, when default occurs, the secured party will exercise his right to repossess the collateral, and most of this chapter will be spent analyzing how he may do this. We shall also examine the secured party's right to a *deficiency judgment*, i.e., his right to recover the difference between what the repossessed property nets on resale and the total amount of the debtor's debt. And we shall examine the debtor's right to various kinds of damages if the secured party does not follow the rules for repossession and resale laid down in the Code.

I. DEFINING DEFAULT

A. Definition left to the parties: Article 9 does not define the term "default". Instead, the parties, in the security agreement, may define "default" more or less as they wish. Since security agreements are typically drawn by the secured party, they will normally contain a long list of events constituting "default", including not only the debtor's failure to make a payment, but also the debtor's bankruptcy, an assignment by him for the benefit of creditors, damage to or removal of the collateral, the debtor's failure to maintain insurance on the collateral, etc.

    1. Acceleration Clause: In addition, the security agreement will usually contain a provision that upon the occurrence of an event or default, the entire sum due to the secured party will become payable *immediately*. Such a provision is called an *acceleration* clause, since full payment of the debt is accelerated.

        a. Significance: The significance of an acceleration clause is that it enables the secured party to treat the entire debt as due at the time of repossession. He is therefore able to sue for a deficiency judgment based upon the difference between the overall debt existing as of the repossession (i.e., the accelerated amount) and the sum netted by resale of the repossessed collateral. Deficiency judgments are further discussed below.

II. CREDITOR'S OPTIONS ON DEFAULT

A. Several options: When an event of default has occurred, the secured party may choose from among several courses of action allowed him by Article 9. These include the following principal plans of attack:

1. **Repossession:** He may make a ***self-help repossession*** of the collateral without invoking judicial process;

2. **Lawsuit:** He may bring a ***lawsuit*** for the amount due (which, if there is an acceleration clause, will be the entire remaining debt); once he obtains judgment, he can then get the sheriff to levy not only on the collateral, but upon any other property of the debtor;

3. **Judicial repossession:** In nearly all states, a secured party can bring an action for judicial repossession (usually called an action in ***replevin*** or for "claim and delivery".) Unlike a lawsuit for the full remaining debt, the action for judicial repossession gets the secured party only the collateral. But it is often easier to obtain procedurally than is a judgment for the full debt, and is sometimes used where self-help is not available because it would constitute "a breach of the peace" (defined below).

4. **Collection:** Where the collateral consists of "accounts" (see *supra*, p. 50), the secured party has the right to notify the "account debtor" (i.e., the person who owes money to the debtor) that he is from now on to pay the secured party and not the debtor. (§9-502(1)).

> **Example:** Car Dealer sells a car to Buyer on credit. Buyer signs a contract with Dealer in which he grants a security interest in the car, and agrees to make monthly payments. Dealer then takes out a loan from Bank, and gives Bank a security interest with Buyer's repayment contract as collateral. If Dealer defaults in its repayments to Bank, Bank may notify Buyer that he is to make payments from now on to Bank, not Dealer.

III. SELF-HELP REPOSSESSION

A. Allowed by Code: The right of self-help repossession is given to the secured party by §9-503: "Unless otherwise agreed a secured party has on default the right to take possession of the collateral. In taking possession, the secured party may proceed without judicial process if this can be done without breach of the peace. . . ."

B. What constitutes "breach of the peace": There is a great body of case law on what constitutes ***"breach of the peace"***. See W&S pp. 1094-1102. A rough summary of the circumstances in which self-help repossession does and does not constitute a breach of the peace is as follows:

1. **Entry onto debtor's premises:** The secured party may not normally enter the debtor's ***home or business*** without permission. This is true whether the debtor is present or not, and whether the premises are locked or not. But see *Cherno v. Bank of Babylon*, 282 N.Y.S. 2d 114 (Sup. Ct. 1967), *aff'd* 288 N.Y.S. 2d 862 (2d Dept.

1968) (upholding the secured party's entry into the debtor's business premises when the debtor was not present, by means of a key procured without the debtor's consent).

2. **Removal of car:** The secured party will usually be allowed to *remove a car* from the debtor's driveway or the street without the debtor's consent (as long as the debtor does not actively protest, a situation described below). Even the "jump-starting" of the car from the debtor's driveway in the middle of the night, or when the debtor is not home, would probably be upheld.

3. **Consent by debtor:** If the debtor *consents* to repossession, there is obviously no breach of peace. But if this consent is procured by a deceptive stratagem (e.g., the secured party or his employees pretend to be policemen), the consent may be held ineffective.

4. **Consent of third person:** If the debtor is not present, an adult who holds a close business or personal relationship with him may be held capable of giving a consent that would render the repossession valid. But consent by the debtor's tenant, landlord, or minor child will not normally be enough to permit entry onto the premises and repossession.

5. **Opposition to repossession:** If the situation is one where an affirmative consent by the debtor is necessary (e.g., entry into the debtor's house to procure the item), the debtor does not have to make a strong opposition to bar repossession; he simply has to refuse to consent. But where the debtor's consent is not necessary (e.g., repossession of a car on the street), it is unclear how much the debtor must do to bar repossession.

   a. **Oral protest:** Most courts hold even an "unequivocal oral protest" by the debtor is enough to create a breach of the peace. (W&S, p. 1100). But other courts require more than words; even in these courts, however, a half-hearted physical attempt to bar repossession would probably be sufficient.

      i. **Superior physical strength and obviously futile protest:** Suppose that it is obvious to the debtor that any attempts to stop the repossession will be futile, because of the superior physical resources and/or hostile attitude of the repossessors. In this situation, there is likely to be a close factual question about whether there has been a breach of the peace. For instance, in *Williams v. Ford Motor Credit Co.*, 674 F.2d 717 (8th Cir. 1982), the debtor was a single mother living in a trailer with her two young children. At 4:30 one morning, she discovered two men in a tow truck beginning to tow her car. She asserted that she was trying to get the payments brought up to date. The repossessors handed her her personal items from the car and then towed it away. The appellate court held that this was not a breach of the peace because the debtor did not strenuously object. But a dissent argued that "where the invasion is detected and a confrontation ensues, the repossessors should be under a duty to retreat and turn to judicial process. The alternative which the majority embraces is to allow a repossessor to proceed following confrontation unless and until violence results in fact. Such a rule invites tragic consequences which the law should seek to prevent, not to encourage."

    b. Better view: The better view seems to be that espoused by White & Summers: "A rule that an oral protest is sufficient to foreclose non-judicial repossession is wise because it does not beckon the repossessing creditor to the brink of violence." W&S, 1101.

C. Constitutionality of self-help repossession: Since the U.S. Supreme Court's decision in *Fuentes v. Shevin*, 92 S.Ct. 1983 (1972), invalidating the kind of *ex parte* "replevin" statutes traditionally used by most states, several debtors have argued that §9-503's self-help repossession provision is also **unconstitutional**. The Supreme Court has not yet ruled on this argument, but the lower courts that have considered the issue have virtually all upheld §9-503 on the ground that it does not involve "state action". Most commentators have argued that the striking down of the self-help repossession provision would benefit only lawyers; See W&S, p. 1085, n. 2.

IV. RESALE OF THE COLLATERAL

A. Resale usual method: Once the secured party has repossessed the collateral, he has the choice between reselling it (in which case he will be able to recover a deficiency judgment against the debtor, for the difference between the resale price and the debt) or with the debtor's consent, taking the collateral in "strict foreclosure" (discussed below), in which case he has no obligation to resell it and can obtain no deficiency. Most of the time, the secured party will elect to resell the collateral. If he does so, he must follow the procedures laid down in §9-504.

B. Substance of §9-504: §9-504(1) allows the secured party wide scope in disposing of the collateral; he may "sell, lease or otherwise dispose of any or all of the collateral in its then condition or following any commercially reasonable preparation or processing." However, the disposition of the collateral is subject to several restrictions, generally for the debtor's benefit:

    1. "Commercially reasonable": All aspects of the disposition must be *"commercially reasonable"* (§9-504(3));

2. **Notice:** The debtor must normally be given *notice* of the "time and place" of sale if the sale is to be a public one, and of the "time after which" any private sale is to occur. (§9-504(3));

3. **Accounting for surplus:** If the disposition yields more than the remaining debt (after the expenses of repossession and resale have been subtracted), the surplus must be given to the debtor. (§9-504(2)).

C. **Disposition must be "commercially reasonable":** The secured party has a choice between a public sale and a private one. (§9-504(3)). The sale or public disposition "may be as a unit or in parcels and at any time and place and on any terms . . . " (*Ibid*). But, and most importantly, " . . . every aspect of the disposition including the method, manner, time, place and terms must be *commercially reasonable*." (*Ibid*).

1. **Insufficient price not determinative:** The requirement that all aspects of the disposition be "commercially reasonable" is a substitute for a requirement that an adequate price be obtained. §9-507(2) expressly states that "the fact that a better price could have been obtained by a sale at a different time or in a different method from that selected by the secured party is not of itself sufficient to establish that the sale was not made in a commercially reasonable manner." However, the adequacy of the price is probably nonetheless an important *sub rosa* consideration in most of the cases construing the term "commercially reasonable". See *Savage Construction v. Challenge-Cook, infra*, p. 162.

   a. **Size of gap:** If the debtor can show that the amount realized on resale was less than half, or even less than three-fourths, of the fair market value of the collateral, he will have a good chance of having the sale held to have been not "commercially reasonable". See e.g., *Atlas Construction Co. v. Dravo-Doyle Co.*, 3 UCC Rep. Serv. 124 (Pa. C.P. 1965) (sale held commercially unreasonable where it yielded 75% of what a handbook for used equipment showed to be the fair market value of the collateral).

2. **Wholesale v. retail:** The Code itself does not state whether the adequacy of the resale is to be gauged against the wholesale market or the retail one. However, Comment 2 to §9-507 indicates that, at least if the secured party does not have the facilities for making retail sales, the wholesale market is the relevant standard of comparison: "One recognized method of disposing of repossessed collateral is for the secured party to sell the collateral to or through a dealer — a method which in the long run may realize better average returns since the secured party does not usually maintain his own facilities for making such sales."

a. Resale expenses subtracted: The rationale behind this statement is that the secured party is entitled, for purposes of calculating the deficiency or surplus, to subtract "the reasonable expenses of . . . selling, leasing and the like. . . ."

Example: Finance Co. repossesses a car from Buyer. Finance Co. will almost certainly be permitted to resell the car to a used-car dealer, and will not be required to resell it at retail. If, however, the secured party were himself a used-car dealer, he would probably be required to resell at retail, rather than to another dealer.

3. **Self-dealing by secured creditor:** Any sign of *self-dealing* or unfairness by the secured creditor is likely to produce a finding that the sale was not "commercially reasonable." For instance, if the secured creditor "bids in" the property at a sparsely-attended public auction, then resells it for substantially more money soon thereafter, the disposition is likely not to be found commercially reasonable. Similarly, the fact that the secured party has *not notified* specific possible bidders who are known to be interested makes it more likely that a public sale was not commercially reasonable.

Example: Debtor defaults on its installment contract with S, a secured party, for the purchase of four cement mixers. S repossesses the equipment and publishes notice of the impending public sale in three publications. S is the only bidder at the action, and purchases the equipment for $158,000. Two weeks later, S sells the four mixers for approximately $200,000. One of those who bought from S had been negotiating with S for the mixers before the public sale, but was not invited to attend and bid.

Held, the public sale was not commercially reasonable. While there is no requirement that the highest possible price be obtained at a public auction, the secured party is obligated to hold the sale under conditions reasonably calculated to bring the fair market value. The price obtained at a retail sale within two weeks of the auction is an indicator of fair market value. Furthermore, the fact that no one attended the public sale implies inadequate publication and/or bad faith on the part of S. Finally, and perhaps most important, S breached its duty when it failed to tell known potential buyers about the auction. *Savage Construction, Inc. v. Challenge-Cook Bros., Inc.,* 714 P.2d 573 (Nev. 1986).

4. **Public vs. private sale:** If the secured party decides to proceed by private, rather than public, sale, he should procure more than one bid.

a. Public sale distinguished from private one: The Code itself does not give a test for distinguishing between a "public" sale and a "private" one. However, Comment 4 to §2-706 states that for Article 2 purposes, "by 'public' sale is meant a sale by auction." Since Comment 1 to §9-504 refers to §2-706 for determining when a sale is "commercially reasonable", an auction would seem to be necessary for a public sale under Article 9 above. However, White & Summers (p. 1121) suggest that *sealed bids*, if solicited through a reasonable amount of publicity, should also be considered to give rise to a "public" sale.

b. Significance of distinction: A choice between a public or private sale has two consequences. First, the notice requirements are different (a distinction discussed below). Secondly, the secured party may bid at a public sale, but at a private sale he may keep the collateral (in effect, purchasing from himself) only if the collateral "is of a type customarily sold in a recognized market or is of a type which is the subject of widely distributed standard price quotations . . ." (§9-504(3)).

    i. Stocks, bonds and commodities: The various national stock exchanges, and the bond and commodity markets, are "recognized markets", and stocks, bonds and commodities traded on them may therefore be bought by the secured party in what is in reality a purchase from himself. The debtor receives protection from an unfair price (and consequent deficiency) by the fact that the fair market value of the items can be determined by checking the national quotations.

    ii. Used cars: On the other hand, used cars, as well as any other kind of used consumer goods, are generally held not to be either "sold in a recognized market" or "the subject of widely distributed standard price quotations". Therefore, the secured party may not buy these items from himself at a private sale.

5. Time within which sale must occur: The Code imposes *no time limit* within which the resale of the collateral must occur. Thus as long as the secured party waits no more than a "commercially reasonable" time, he does not have to hurry to dispose of the goods.

    a. Exception: The sole exception to this general rule is given by §9-505(1), which provides that where the collateral is "consumer goods", and the debtor has paid 60% or more of either the cash price (in the case of a purchase money security interest) or of the loan (in non-purchase money cases), the secured party must make the sale within *90 days after repossession*. This obligation can be waived by the debtor only *after* default. If the disposition does not occur within 90 days, the debtor has the option of bringing an action for conversion, or recovering statutory damages set by §9-507(1) (discussed below).

6. Payment by guarantor not disposition: Normally, it will not be difficult to determine whether the secured party has disposed of the collateral, as §9-504 requires him to do. But if the secured party has obtained a *guarantee* of the indebtedness which the security interest secures, an ambiguity can arise with respect to when disposition has occurred.

   a. Subrogation: When default occurs, the guarantor is obligated to pay the amount of the debt. If he does so, he becomes *subrogated* to the secured party's rights, and he himself becomes a secured party. (§9-504(5)).

   b. Not a sale or disposition: When such a payment by the guarantor, and consequent subrogation, occurs, the transfer of collateral to the guarantor is *not considered to be a sale or disposition*, under a special provision of §9-504(5). The guarantor thus bears the burden of disposing of the collateral anew under §9-504. The same rules apply to a person who has endorsed the note representing the indebtedness, and to one who has agreed to *repurchase* the collateral.

   Example: Dealer sells a car under a conditional sales contract to Buyer. Dealer then sells the contract to Bank, but agrees that upon default by Buyer, he will repurchase the contract from Bank. Buyer defaults, Bank repossesses, and Dealer repurchases the contract (and receives the car) from Bank. By so doing, Dealer is subrogated to all the rights of Bank, and now has a security interest in the car. But under §9-504(5), Bank is not deemed to have made a "sale or disposition" of the collateral, and Dealer must in turn sell or dispose of the collateral under §9-504.

D. Application of proceeds: Once the sale or other disposition has occurred, the secured party is entitled to take off the top "the reasonable expenses of retaking, holding, preparing for sale or lease, selling, leasing and the like and, to the extent provided for in the agreement and not prohibited by law, the reasonable attorneys' fees and legal expenses incurred by [him]." (§9-504(1)(a)).

   1. Significance: The practical importance of this provision is that these expenses of repossession and disposition are subtracted from any surplus which might otherwise be due to the debtor, and are added to any deficiency which he owes.

E. Notice of resale: The debtor, and in some instances other secured parties, must usually be *notified* of the proposed sale. (§9-504(3)).

1. **When notice to debtor need not be given:** There are three circumstances when notice to the debtor *need not be given*:

    a. **Perishables:** if the collateral is "perishable or threatens to decline speedily in value" (e.g., tomatoes) (§9-504(3)); or

    b. **Recognized market:** if the collateral "is of a type customarily sold on a recognized market"; (stocks, bonds and commodities traded on a national exchange would fall within this category, but used cars or other used hard goods would not); or

    c. **Waiver of right to notice:** under the present Code, (but not the 1962 Code), if the debtor has "signed *after default* a statement renouncing or modifying his right to notification of sale."

2. **Who is a "debtor":** Notice must be sent to the "debtor". But under §9-105(1)(d), "debtor" is defined to include one who "owes payment or other performance of the obligation secured. . . ." Where there is a guarantor or endorser in addition to the owner of the collateral, they must be both treated as "debtors" for notice purposes, and must thus both be notified. However, as the following examples illustrates, the issue of who is a "debtor" is not always a straightforward one.

    Example: Dealer sells a used car to Goldsmith, a consumer. Goldsmith buys on credit, giving Dealer a security interest and a promissory note. Dealer sells the note and security agreement (which together constitute "chattel paper" — see §9-105(1)(b)) to Bank. As part of the sale of the paper, Dealer agrees that if Goldsmith defaults, he will repurchase the paper from Bank. Goldsmith defaults, but Bank, instead of asking Dealer to repurchase the chattel paper, repossesses the car, sells it for less than the price at which Dealer would have been obligated to repurchase the paper (without giving Dealer notice of the sale), and sues Dealer for the difference. Dealer argues that he was a "debtor" under §9-105(1)(d) because he owed "payment, *or other performance* of the obligation", namely, the duty to repurchase the papers, and that he was therefore entitled to notice before the car was sold, under §9-504(3).

    Held, Dealer was indeed a debtor, and was entitled to notice. The Court rejected the argument contained in an *amicus curiae* brief submitted by the UCC Permanent Editorial board, to the effect that there were *two* security interests, an interest in chattel paper and an interest in the car, that Dealer was a debtor only as to the paper, and that he was not entitled to notice under §9-504(3) before resale of the car.

(The court refused to hold that the lack of notice discharged Dealer entirely; instead, it held that this lack shifted the burden of establishing the fairness of the resale price from Dealer to Bank. See p. 155 for a discussion of various judicial positions on whether a secured party's failure to follow the Article 9 default procedure automatically deprives him of the right to a deficiency judgment.) See *Norton v. National Bank of Commerce*, 398 S.W.2d 538 (Ark. 1966)

3. **Notice to secured parties:** Where the collateral is consumer goods, notice to the debtor is the only notice required. (§9-504(3)). But in all other cases, certain other **secured parties** must be given notice of the sale or other disposition. The class of secured parties who must be notified depends on whether the 1962 Code, or the present Code, is in effect.

   a. **Old Code:** Under the 1962 code, notice must be given to any other secured party who either:

      i. filed a financing statement under the debtor's name in the state where the notice-giving secured party's interest is filed; or

      ii. is "known by the secured party to have a security interest in the collateral."

   b. **Present Code:** The above two requirements compel secured parties operating under the original Code to both conduct a search of the files and public records for other security interests, and to search their own records for evidence of letters, phone calls, etc. that might disclose the existence of other security interests. This was felt to be unreasonably burdensome, since senior secured parties do not normally need the protection that notice would give (the collateral would be sold subject to their superior security interests anyway), and "as a practical matter there would seldom be a junior secured party who really had an interest needing protection in the case of a foreclosure sale." (§9-504, "Reasons for 1972 Change").

      i. **New Rule:** Therefore, under the present Code, notice need be given only to "any other secured party from whom the secured party has received (before sending his notification to the debtor or before the debtor's renunciation of his rights) **written notice of a claim** of an interest in the collateral." In other words, the junior secured party, at the time he takes his interest, bears the burden of notifying the senior secured party that he now has an interest in the same collateral.

4. **Requirement of a writing:** Most cases held that *oral* notice by the foreclosing secured party to the debtor and other secured parties is *insufficient*. This view is corroborated by the fact that §9-504(3) requires that notice be "sent", and "send" is defined in §1-201(38) as meaning "to deposit in the mail or deliver for transmission by any other usual means of communication. . . ." A telephone or face-to-face oral message would not seem to fit within this language. (See W&S, p. 1112). However, there are cases holding an oral notice to be sufficient; See W&S, p. 1112, n. 105.

   a. **Receipt not necessary:** It is not necessary, however, that the debtor actually *receive* the notification. "If the mailman loses the notice or the debtor's wife throws it in the wastebasket, that is the debtor's tough luck" (W&S, p. 1112).

5. **Contents of notice:** What information the notice must contain depends on whether a sale is to be a public one or a private one.

   a. **Public sale:** If the sale is to be public, the notice must contain the "time and place" of the sale. §9-504(3)).

   b. **Private sale:** Where the sale is to be private, on the other hand, the notice only has to state "the time after which any private sale or other intended disposition is to be made." (*Ibid*).

6. **Time:** The Code does not state how long before the proposed sale the notice must be sent. However, Comment 5 to §9-504 states that "at a minimum [the notice] must be sent in such time that persons entitled to receive it will have sufficient time to take appropriate steps to protect their interests by taking part in the sale or other disposition if they so desire."

   a. **Interpretation:** White and Summers state that this Comment should be interpreted to mean that the creditor must mail the notice at such a time that he would "reasonably expect it to arrive in the debtor's hands in time to give him several business days in which to arrange alternative financing." (W&S, p. 1114). A week's notice will almost always be sufficient. (*ibid*). (Remember, also, that the issue is not how much notice is actually received, but how much notice the creditor reasonably *thought* he was giving to the debtor, regardless of when the debtor actually receives the communication.)

V. DEBTOR'S RIGHT TO REDEEM COLLATERAL

A. **Right of redemption generally:** At any time between default and the eventual disposition of the collateral by the secured party, the debtor has a right to *redeem* the collateral by paying the secured party "all obligations secured by the collateral" plus "the expenses reasonably incurred by the secured party in retaking, holding and preparing the collateral for disposition, in arranging for the sale, and to the extent provided in the agreement and not prohibited by law, his reasonable attorneys' fees and legal expenses." (§9-506).

B. Acceleration clause: If the security agreement contains an acceleration clause, as almost all do, the debtor must, in order to redeem the collateral, tender the *entire balance*, not just the amount by which he was in arrears at the time of repossession. (Official Comment to §9-506).

C. Not waivable after defaults: The debtor cannot waive his right to redemption prior to default. But once default has occurred, the debtor may waive his right of redemption provided that he does so in writing. (§9-506).

D. Strict foreclosure: The right of redemption is cut off not only by a disposition of the collateral by the secured party but also by any agreement between the debtor and secured party that the collateral will be taken in full satisfaction of the debt (i.e., the device of "strict foreclosure", discussed immediately below).

VI. TAKING THE COLLATERAL FOR THE DEBT ("STRICT FORECLOSURE")

A. The concept generally: Normally, the secured party will resell the collateral under §9-504; if the sale does not net enough to cover the expenses of repossession and resale plus the debtor's outstanding balance, the secured party may recover a deficiency judgment against the debtor for the difference. This right to a deficiency judgment is given by §9-504(2). But since a resale under §9-504 must follow the somewhat technical rules set out above, and since the secured party is liable for a variety of penalties if he fails to obey them (discussed below), he may sometimes prefer to simply "take the collateral for the debt". That is, he will be willing to forego any right to a deficiency judgment, in return for not having to follow the procedures of §9-504, and not having to account to the debtor for any surplus. The taking of the collateral in full satisfaction of the debt is sometimes called *"strict foreclosure"*.

B. When available: If the security interest involves consumer goods, and the debtor has paid 60% of the loan or cash price, strict foreclosure is not available, unless the debtor has signed *after default* a statement modifying his right to insist upon a resale. (§9-505(1)). In all other cases, the secured party may propose strict foreclosure. To do so, he must take the following steps:

1. **Repossession:** First, he must repossess the collateral. (§9-505(1));

2. **Written proposal:** Then, he must "propose to retain the collateral in satisfaction of the obligation." This proposal must be in writing, and must be shown to the debtor, unless he has renounced this right after default, §9-505(2). In the case of consumer goods, no one else is entitled to notice. But in non-consumer goods situations, notice of the proposal must also be sent to any other secured party who has previously given notice to a claim to the collateral (i.e., anyone who would have been entitled to notice of sale under §9-504(3)). §9-505(2).

3. **Waiting period:** Finally, the secured party must wait 21 days. If no objection is received to the strict foreclosure proposal, the secured party may retain the collateral in satisfaction of the debt. But if either the debtor or a secured party entitled to notice makes a *written* objection within 21 days from sending of the notice, the secured party must sell or otherwise dispose of the collateral under §9-504, and cannot retain it in satisfaction of the debt.

C. **Where 60% of debt paid by consumer debtor:** As noted above, where the collateral is consumer goods, and the debtor has paid 60% of the debt (either 60% of the cash price in the case of a purchase money security interest, or 60% of the loan in all other cases) strict foreclosure is not available unless the debtor signs, after default, a statement "renouncing or modifying" his right to insist on disposition. In other words, the debtor's failure to respond within 30 days with a written objection, which would be sufficient to allow strict foreclosure in all other situations, is not sufficient in this 60%-payment situation. But if the debtor signs the appropriate renunciation or modification of his rights, strict foreclosure may nonetheless occur. The theory behind this provision is that once the debtor has built up 60% equity in the goods, it should be presumed that he would not willingly sacrifice his chance to obtain a surplus. (Recall that under §9-504(2)), "the secured party must account to the debtor for any surplus. . . .")

D. **Debtor forces strict foreclosure on secured creditor:** Suppose that the secured creditor does not send notice that he is pursuing strict foreclosure, but he repossesses the collateral and *delays* in re-selling it and/or uses it himself. If the secured party then comes after the debtor for a deficiency, the debtor may claim that the secured party's *actions*, even in the absence of notice of strict foreclosure, constituted an *implied* strict foreclosure, so that the debtor cannot be required to pay a deficiency. If the delay in re-selling the collateral is substantial, or the secured party has made substantial use of the collateral himself, the court is likely to accept the debtor's argument that there has been an implied strict foreclosure.

Example: Secured Party has a security interest in a truck owned by Debtors. Debtors default, and Secured Party repossesses the truck in December 1979. Secured Party repairs the truck by May 1980, and unsuccessfully attempts to sell it. Secured Party then leases it to others for the next three years, during which time it is driven over 200,000 miles. Secured Party never gives Debtors a notice of intent to use strict foreclosure. Secured Party finally sells the truck in April 1983 for less than the outstanding debt, and sues Debtors for the resulting deficiency.

Held, for Debtors. It is true that Secured Party did not give notice of an intent to take the property in strict foreclosure. But by using it for nearly three years, and by causing it to be operated for 200,000 miles, Secured Party implicitly elected to use strict foreclosure and thus waived his right to a deficiency. *Schmode's Inc. v. Wilkinson*, 361 N.W.2d 557 (Neb. 1985).

Note: Virtually all courts would hold that substantial actual use of the collateral by the secured party of the collateral, as in *Schmode's*, is enough to constitute an implied strict foreclosure. Where the only act by the secured party that arguably constitutes strict foreclosure is the long passage of time before a sale, courts disagree about whether strict foreclosure should be found. See W&S, p. 1107.

VII. CONSEQUENCES OF CREDITOR'S FAILURE TO FOLLOW RULES

A. **Consequences generally:** As we have seen, there are at least three respects in which a creditor may fail to follow the rules set forth in the default provisions of Article 9. He may breach the peace in repossessing; he may fail to give the proper notice of resale; or he may fail to dispose of the collateral in a "commercially reasonable" manner. If he does any of these things, he may be stricken by one or more of at least five ill consequences:

1. Criminal liability;

2. Tort liability;

3. Liability under §9-507 for loss caused to the debtor by improper behavior;

4. Minimum penalty damages imposed by §9-507 for improper behavior in consumer goods cases; and

5. Denial of a deficiency judgment.

B. Criminal and tort liability: If the secured party breaches the peace in repossessing, he may incur criminal liability (e.g., assault and battery) under state law. Also, he may have violated the Federal Consumer Credit Protection Act's ban on "extortionate" collection practices (15 U.S.C. §1601-77). Furthermore, he may have incurred tort liability for trespass, assault, battery, conversion, etc.

C. Code liability for loss: Under §9-507(1), the Court is given power both to prevent violations of the default rules before they occur, and to award damages for violations after they occur.

    1. Prevention of violations: Under the first sentence of §9-507(1), "If it is established that the secured party is not proceeding in accordance with the provisions of this Part, disposition may be ordered or restrained on appropriate terms and conditions."

        a. Bankruptcy application: This provision is of particular interest where the debtor has become a bankrupt, and the Court wants to make sure that notice of proposed sale is given to all parties entitled thereto, and that the sale is commercially reasonable.

    2. After disposition: Once the disposition has occurred, "the debtor or any person entitled to notification or whose security interest has been made known to the secured party prior to the disposition has a right to recover from the secured party any loss caused by a failure to comply with the provisions of this Part." (§9-507). If the secured party has repossessed when, as it turns out, no "default" has occurred, damages might include the debtor's loss of profits from his business. If the collateral is resold in a "commercially unreasonable" manner, damages would normally be measured by the difference between the amount actually received on resale and the amount which would have been obtained if the resale had been commercially reasonable. (See W&S, p. 1126).

D. Penalty in consumer goods cases: The measure of damages described immediately above compensates the debtor only for his actual losses. In consumer goods cases, this actual loss will normally be trivial, and the threat of damages based upon it will not usually be enough to deter secured creditors from wrongdoing. Therefore, §9-507 also includes a *minimum penalty in consumer goods cases:* "if the collateral is consumer goods, the debtor has a right to recover in any event an amount not less than the credit service charge plus 10 percent of the principal amount of the debt or the time price differential plus 10 percent of the cash price."

    1. Explanation: In other words, where the secured party is a merchant who has sold the goods on credit, the penalty is the difference between the price of the item when bought on credit and its price when bought for cash, plus 10% of this cash price; when the secured party is a lender (e.g., a finance company), the penalty is the entire interest on the loan plus 10% of the original principal on the debt.

2. **No actual damages need be proved:** Note that the consumer is entitled to this penalty even if he has not suffered any actual loss at all.

E. **Denial of the deficiency:** In most cases, the most important punishment the creditor may suffer as the result of his violation of the default procedures is the possible *denial of a deficiency judgment*. The courts have varied in their willingness to make an automatic denial of a deficiency where creditor misbehavior has occurred.

1. *Per se* **rule:** Some courts have held that once it is shown that the secured party has violated any of Article 9's default provisions, he is automatically barred from recovering a deficiency. This position was most notably espoused by *Skeels v. Universal CIT Credit Corp.*, 222 F.Supp. 696 (W.D. Pa. 1963), modified on other grounds, 335 F.2d 846 (3d Cir. 1964). The *Skeels* court based its holding on the theory that automatic denial of deficiency is a necessary deterrent to creditor misbehavior.

2. **Accord and satisfaction:** Some courts, principally the Georgia Court of Appeals, have used the theory of "*accord and satisfaction*".

> **Example:** Debtor's sister-in-law drives Debtor's car, in which Finance Company has a security interest, to Finance Company's offices in order to make an overdue payment. Finance Company's employee asks for the keys, to "see whether we have our money's worth in it." He takes a drive in the car, and then informs her, "We are going to keep it." Finance Company then sells the car at a private sale without giving notice to Debtor. It then sues Debtor for a deficiency judgment. *Held*, Finance Company, by taking the car in the surreptitious manner it did, in effect granted an "accord and satisfaction" of debtor's liability, i.e., an agreement that repossession of the car would cancel the indebtedness. See *Moody v. Nides Finance Co.*, 156 S.E.2d 310 (Ga. App. 1967).

3. **Presumption that loss equals amount of deficiency:** Other courts have declined to automatically deny deficiency, but have instead applied a *presumption* that the amount of the debtor's loss equals the amount of the sought-after deficiency. This approach frees the debtor of the burden of proving the amount of his actual loss; but the secured party remains free to prove that the actual loss was minimal, in which case he can still recover the difference between the deficiency and this minimal loss. See, e.g. *Norton v.*

National Bank of Commerce 398 S.W.2d 538 (Ark. 1968).

4. **Offsetting of damages:** Still other courts refuse to apply even the presumption described above, and permit the debtor only to offset against the deficiency the amount of any actual loss he can prove. Since as a practical matter it is generally quite difficult for the debtor to prove substantial losses, this approach gives him cold comfort. See, e.g., *Mercantile Financial Corp. v. Miller*, 292 F.Supp. 797 (E.D. Pa. 1968).

5. **UCCC:** A number of states have enacted the Uniform Consumer Credit Code (UCCC), which, among other things, prohibits any secured party from obtaining a deficiency where he repossesses consumer goods which had a cash sale price of $1,000 or less. See UCCC, §5-103.

TABLE OF CASES

STATUTORY REFERENCES
UNIFORM COMMERCIAL CODE

BANKRUPTCY CODE

SUBJECT MATTER INDEX